Clay in the Primary School

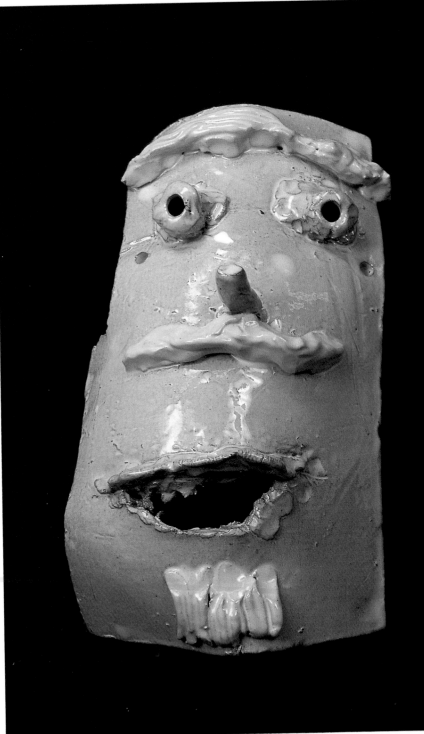

CLAY IN THE PRIMARY SCHOOL

Peter Clough

A & C Black · London

To Chrissie

First published in Great Britain 1996
A & C Black (Publishers) Limited
35 Bedford Row London WC1R 4JH

Copyright © 1996 Peter Clough

ISBN 0–7136–3978–4

Published simultaneously in the US by
Davis Publications, Inc., 50 Portland Street,
Worcester, Massachusetts 01608

A CIP catalogue record for this book is available from
the British Library.

Front: Two ladies with scarf and necklace, Amy,
aged 4 and Natalie, aged 5.
Back: Triceratops by Helen, aged 7. Earthenware,
slip decorated.
Frontispiece: Mask by Richard, aged 7. Earthenware
and stoneware clays. White glaze. 1140°C.

Designed by Alan Hamp
Typeset by August Filmsetting, St Helens, UK
Printed in Hong Kong by Wing King Tong Ltd

Contents

Acknowledgements

I would like to thank John Devine and all the staff at Bilton Grange County Primary School in Harrogate for their support and enthusiasm throughout this project, and particularly Jen Whiteley who was so constantly generous with her time and energy. Thanks also to many others who gave so willingly, including Brenda Wright, Linda McCarthy, Caroline Perry, and Sandra Barlow with their work from Melsonby Methodist Primary School and Ravensworth Church of England School, near Richmond, North Yorkshire; Mollington CE Primary School, Chester; and Menston Primary School, Ilkley, Leeds.

I must also pay tribute to the staff at the Ashmolean Museum, Oxford and the City Museum, Hanley, Stoke on Trent for their assistance with the illustrations from their collections.

Thanks also to Janet Cheesborough and her children for their assistance with the practical photographs.

I am grateful to The University College of Ripon and York St. John for allowing me time to work on this book, and finally thanks must go to all the children for the delight I have had in working with them and for the pleasure and inspiration which their work has given to us all.

Introduction

One September Sunday morning at a Northern Potters Conference I was sitting at breakfast with Chrissie, my wife, and Linda Lambert, the Ceramics editor for A & C Black. The conversation between them turned to primary schools and Chrissie, who has a class of 6 year olds, bemoaned the lack of information for teachers using clay in school. They agreed that this was something which was needed, but who would write it? There was a moment's silence, and they turned to me!

That was the start of a journey which has culminated in this book. It has been a fascinating trip, not without frustrations and effort as any journey usually is, but rewarded by some wonderful moments with teachers, and more especially with the children. Their excitement and enthusiasm in creating the work which is illustrated here has been a driving force and needs no justification from me as to the value of using clay with children.

Since teachers' experience of clay varies enormously, in deciding the contents I have tried to include information which would be of value to both beginners and more experienced practitioners. This is not an easy line to draw, and if you are a beginner and feel overawed, or if you are experienced and feel that I have stated the obvious, please forgive me. I hope that you appreciate the problem.

'It is the journey that counts, not the arrival, the experience, not the result.'

Whatever the argument, I hope that you enjoy the journey as much as I have, that your experience of using clay is as pleasurable and valuable as it has been with my children, and I am sure that the results will exceed your expectations.

Harrogate, 1995

'Happy Man' by Victoria, aged 6. Biscuit fired.

responses by different individuals, and so whatever their age or previous experience they can come to the material at their own level. As with other art media such as drawing materials and paint, clay can be used as a vehicle for the expression of ideas and feelings, and reactions to the environment in which the children find themselves.

In addition, there is the active physical involvement in handling this wonderfully malleable material and the development of manipulative skills through touching, poking, pushing, banging, prodding, squeezing and joining, using knuckles, thumbs and fingers. We are also encouraging the development of skills in handling clay, and through this, insights and confidence which will relate to working and understanding the properties of other materials.

The balance between imagination and skills

When presenting work to children there is a fine line to be drawn between these elements as every teacher will know, and it is a line which will vary depending upon the sort of learning and experience which the teacher decides should take place. At one extreme the child may simply be given the material and asked to play with it, making whatever he wishes. This is a perfectly valid imaginative approach. The child will begin to work, using whatever previous experience he has in terms of handling and forming, discovering for himself what it will do and how it behaves, how it can be joined, and looking at how other children are making as part of a total group experience. Children will generally rely on their own ideas about

Above
Chunky man by Sarah, aged 6. Biscuit fired.

Right
'Me with a Book' by Emma, aged 6. Biscuit fired.

'The owl who couldn't sleep' Group, aged 5.
Slip with transparent e/w glaze.

what they are producing, although they may also take on ideas from others in the group. Many of the small modelled pieces made by younger children in this book were produced in this way. At the other extreme, there is the totally teacher-centred approach which relies on carefully followed technical instruction, resulting in work which has a minimal imaginative input from the child, and which may remain lifeless and dull.

Fortunately, this latter approach is rare, but there is still a need to teach children ways in which they can use clay easily and efficiently to make what they wish, and to understand where the problems are likely to be. For this to happen, there needs to be a sequential programme of experience throughout the primary years which relates to the physical and intellectual development of the child. With clay this may follow the structure of this book, moving from modelling and pinching to coiling, slabwork and so on. These processes, however, overlap in many ways and whilst they do provide some guidelines for the progression and development of skills and understanding, are not given as a sequence written in stone!

What is more important are the ways in which children are effectively taught skills. If they are given widely spaced and random experience in the use of any material, many children have difficulty

Dog, Chinese, Han Dynasty, 206BC–AD220. Stoneware with green glaze. *Courtesy of the Ashmolean Museum.*

in retaining and then recalling and building upon it. It is important that skills once presented, are practised, and the knowledge consolidated, particularly with those who have difficulty in approaching and retaining new ideas and concepts in the first place. In addition, the sequence of three-dimensional activities should be so structured that problems encountered in one project are re-inforced and developed subsequently.

For the teacher, every session should consider where the emphasis will lie and what the content will be. The following questions are provided as a focus for this thinking and assume that the children's stage of development and previous experience are known.

1. What stimulus is going to be used for the work? What story, object, topic etc. will be presented to the children to focus their thinking?
2. What are the links between this stimulus and other areas of the curriculum?
3. What new insights are going to be introduced about clay as a material?
4. What new skills or processes are going to be demonstrated/explained?
5. How will you relate the stimulus to the process, and what freedom will you give the children to develop their ideas in an imaginative and personal way?

6. Will you involve the children in a problem of a visual and/or practical nature which they will need to solve?

These are the basic theoretical planning issues which need to be addressed; the questions about classroom organisation and ways in which the clay can be used are covered later.

Cross curricular links

These, as has already been mentioned, are many and varied but some of the obvious ones are worth drawing out at this point.

History

It is often through the examination and study of archaeological remains that we all develop an appreciation of our own culture and of our cultural heritage, and of course, it is often through the examination of ceramic remains in particular that we gain insights into other cultures and traditions. The use of clay goes back to prehistory and the artefacts produced since then in different parts of the world provide a rich seam of

Cock, Roman, 1st–2nd century AD. *Courtesy of the Ashmolean Museum.*

source material to which children may respond. These artefacts tell us a great deal about the religious and social customs of a period, the ways people lived their daily lives, and much more besides.

A selection of this resource material is included later in the book when practical activities are covered, because it is when children are actively involved with the material that such relationships and stimulus are most relevant. It is for each teacher to select and present material which is appropriate to the particular project.

Geography

The obvious visual link here is the variation in the character of artefacts from different countries around the world. Each is a reflection of a particular culture, shaped by climate, customs and economic circumstances all of which result in a great variety of forms of expression. We are also concerned here with geology which is a fundamental element in ceramics. The ways in which clay is formed, deposited and mined are basic concepts in this area, and are covered in more detail later. Children need to be aware that they are working with a particular kind of earth, that it originates from the ground beneath us, and that glazes are a form of glass which is made from a variety of natural materials most of which are quarried in one form or another. They also need to be aware that there are different types of clay and that we use them for different purposes.

Science

There are a number of scientific concepts which can be introduced and explored

through clay. The principle of change, both reversible and irreversible, is an obvious one, through the processes of soaking, drying and soaking (reversible) and firing (irreversible). There is also the concept that materials can be changed in shape by applying forces such as squeezing, bending, rolling and so on.

Comparisons can be made between clay and other materials in relation to such properties as porosity, hardness, appearance, texture and insulation. The heating of clay can be related to other heating processes such as cooking food and manufacturing glass and metals. The differences between red heat and white heat can also be considered.

Mathematics

Changes in weight and size can be measured as the clay changes from plastic and dry to the fired state, and by using a given weight of clay and seeing who can make the largest, tallest, widest vessel. Once fired, estimates can be made about how much a vessel will hold, and it can then be filled and the results checked. Similarly, work can be conducted into the comparative weights of pieces using both estimates and scales. Children involved in more advanced work with slabs will also probably need to plan and measure their work carefully as part of the making process.

Design and technology

There are considerable overlaps here with other areas of the curriculum, notably art, science and mathematics. The ways in which these are drawn out as part of children's understandings will depend very much on the focus of the lesson and the emphasis by the teacher. Clearly, any experience of working clay will need to be related to the working and shaping of other materials, and children in any case will instinctively use manipulative skills developed with one material and relate them to others. There are, however, some important educational questions which need to be addressed in this area. Teachers need to consider carefully where the balance will lie between open-ended, creative exploration on the one hand, and a design based problem-solving approach on the other. In practice, most lessons will contain some elements of both of these including on occasion discussion about structure, function and the evaluation of a variety of ceramic and other objects.

Clay in the environment

An awareness of the many uses to which clay is put, both now and in the past, must go hand in hand with children's experience of using the material. We are all familiar as adults with many of the common applications, but there is a wide conceptual gap for children between the soft grey or red substance which comes out of a plastic bag or bin in the classroom, and the enormous variety of

forms, colours and uses which we find in the fired state in our everyday surroundings. We need to draw children's attention to this as part of a full and wide-ranging experience, and to ensure that they are visually alert to this aspect of their daily life. We should encourage an understanding of the practical uses of clay by looking around the home and school. Here we find cups, mugs, bowls and vases in daily use with smooth glossy surfaces in a variety of colours. On the walls and floors are tiles of different colours, and possibly also different shapes. The toilets and washbasins may be made from clay, as in all probability will be the underground drains. Outside we find bricks, some new, some old, with a variety of colours, sizes, textures and weights, depending upon how they were made and fired. Sometimes these are laid in patterns to enrich and decorate the walls. On the roof there may well be flat clay tiles, but sometimes curved pantiles are found, and with colours ranging from terracotta to a deep blue-grey. The visual quality of these objects will vary, depending upon the function of the form, the type of clay, glazing and firing, and also whether it

Old handmade brick.

New pressed brick

has been made by a machine or by hand.

We have the opportunity then, in using clay with our children, to develop an enormous wealth of insights and understanding across much of the primary curriculum, to encourage and develop relationships and links in children's knowledge, and to provide the opportunity for individual creative response and discovery. It should be remembered that in all of this, as every primary teacher knows, there is no substitute for direct, hands-on experience.

Chapter Two
Clay, the Material

What clay is made from

Children are innately curious and you are bound to be asked where clay comes from, and from what it is made. The fact that there might be clay underneath the school is something which could be

pointed out, since clay in one form or another covers much of the earth's surface. How it is formed and an understanding of the different qualities of clay requires more careful explanation, and the ways in which this is done will naturally depend upon the age of the children.

In essence, all clay originates as either

Mining clay.

igneous or metamorphic rock, which is then broken down by water and ice to form clays with different characteristics. From igneous rock, or granite, we get a very pure clay, e.g. china clay or kaolinite, whilst from combinations of igneous and metamorphic rock we obtain a similar clay, but which has a more complex structure, and which contains more chemical elements. Primary clays are found where they are formed, and the china clay of south-west England near St. Austell is a good example of this. The rock has been broken down by weathering over a long period of time and the clay has remained in that area. Since it has not been contaminated by other materials it remains a white or creamy colour.

Secondary clays, however, are transported from their place of origin, usually by ice and water, and then deposited elsewhere. This washing away of the decomposed rock allows the clay particles to be ground to a finer size, and when they settle, the coarser particles sink to the bottom, giving a variation in the composition of the clay. These secondary clays are very important because it is from these highly plastic, fine clays that we obtain the material which we use in school. The colour of the raw clay may vary from light grey to a deep red, depending upon the volume of iron and other impurities picked up during transportation.

Some of these deposits can be used for making pottery with little further work, but often they require blending with other clays and minerals to render them suitable for particular making or firing processes. When this is done, they are called 'bodies', and the suppliers catalogues contain many different clays for use in a wide variety of situations. We will consider the selection of the most suitable clay later. Before we do this, some explanation of the structure of clay bodies is useful, because this has a fundamental effect on how successful the children will be when they are working with it.

I have mentioned plasticity already, but the strength and plasticity of a particular clay is extremely important in determining the way in which it will work. The finer the particle size, the more plastic it will be. China clay and some fireclays have a coarse particle size, and are therefore very 'short' or 'lean' with low plasticity. In order to use china clay in, for example, porcelain bodies, it has to be blended with other minerals such as feldspar and extremely plastic clays like bentonite. The secondary clays, ball clay, some fireclays, and earthenware clays are often already very fine and plastic, and are called 'fat' or 'long' clays. The differences in these clays are due to the crystal structure, and since this has such profound influence on the working properties it is

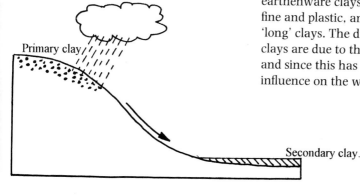

Primary clay

Secondary clay.

Formation of clay

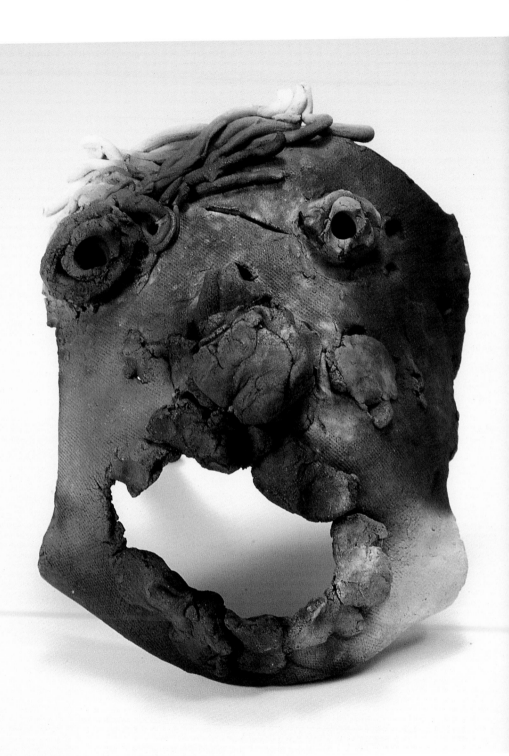

Mask by Christopher, aged 6. Earthenware and stoneware clay, smoke-fired.

necessary to understand a little of this for our work with children.

Clay is made up of microscopic flat and roughly hexagonal crystals which are smallest in ball clay and secondary clays, and largest in china clay. Even so, the smallest speck of clay dust will be made up of many hundreds of crystals, and these are invisible to the naked eye. In between these particles is water, which acts as a lubricant and allows them to slide over each other. As the water evaporates, the clay crystals come closer together, and the clay becomes harder and more brittle, eventually cracking when worked. In practical terms then, it is important that the clay retains this water content for as long as possible when children are working, and both the teacher and children must be alert to this as a problem. Suggestions for controlling the moisture content of clay occur in later chapters.

The stages through which clay goes during drying are: plastic, to leather-hard, to greenware, and to bone dry. *Leatherhard* is the state when the clay is firm enough to be picked up without bending, when the crystals are just touching, and when the clay will take a polish with a smooth tool. *Greenware* is the state when the clay has been allowed to dry out completely ready for firing. There will still be a small amount of moisture retained in the pores of the clay, but no further work can be done to the form, which is now hard, but very brittle. The *bone dry* state occurs during the early part of the firing cycle when the clay reaches 100°C (212°F) and the atmospheric moisture retained in the clay is driven off.

Almost all of the work which we do with children occurs when the clay is plastic or soft leatherhard, and this is the time when moisture loss is most rapid.

During the drying and firing process all clays shrink. Most of this shrinkage occurs up to the greenware state, when a clay might shrink between 5%–8%, with further shrinkage during the firing giving a total shrinkage from start to finish of between 11%–13%. This does not usually cause too many problems with children, unless a very dense clay which has a thick section is allowed to dry out quickly, which can lead to drying cracks.

Before we can decide on the selection of the most suitable clay for our

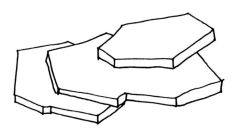

Clay crystals

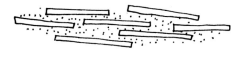

Plastic clay with water between crystals.

Hard clay.

Plastic and hard clay structure

classroom work, we need to consider the general categories of clay types, which for most practical considerations in school divide into either earthenware or stoneware.

Earthenware

This is the commonest clay, and the one most likely to be found in the vicinity of any school. It is usually reddish-brown, although it may also have a yellow ochre or black-brown colour, depending upon the amount and type of iron contamination. It is a dense clay, very plastic, and remains porous when fired which means that it requires a glaze all over if it is to hold liquid. The lower glaze firing temperature of between 1060°C (1940°F) and 1140°C (2048°F) permits a wide range of colour in the glaze, which normally has a good bright shiny surface.

Stoneware

This is usually a grey or buff colour in the natural state, and will fire to a much higher temperature than earthenware, between 1200°C (2192°F) and 1300°C (2372°F). This higher temperature produces a very hard and strong product, which is often vitrified and which, because it has a low porosity, will hold liquids.

In a glaze firing the body and the glaze mature at the same time, forming a body-glaze layer which gives a distinctive soft and mottled appearance to the glaze surface. The colours also tend to be more muted and earthy, with browns, greens, ochres and blacks predominating, although recent developments in ceramic technology have increased the palette of colours available. Within the category of

stonewares, there are a variety of other clays in common use, including porcelain, china, salt glaze and ovenware, all characterised by their different uses and appearance, and all fired to a high temperature. In practical terms, this has little effect on the average classroom claywork because these more specialist clays are not likely to be used, but in terms of a wider understanding of ceramics we need to make the children aware of them as part of their environment.

Selecting the right clay for your children

It is absolutely essential that the clay which you give to the children is the right one for the work which they are going to do, and I make no apology for mentioning this frequently throughout this book.

There are four questions which you need to ask and answer as a teacher.

1. What type of clay am I going to use – Earthenware or Stoneware?
In terms of working properties there is likely to be little to choose between these two clays, but if you require the warm red colour of earthenware then this will be an obvious choice. It is useful to have available both clays, because older children may have individual preferences when it comes to selecting the material to realise their ideas and with care it is possible to use them in combination to provide a colour contrast.

2. What state is the clay in?
This is of paramount importance for success. The teacher needs to develop an instinctive feel when handling the clay for what it will allow the children to make. The clay must be neither too sticky nor too firm. It is preferable in a

warm classroom for the clay to be a little too soft to begin with, as it will begin to firm up within half an hour as it starts to dry. If it is too firm, then the clay will be more difficult to work and will begin to crack before the children have finished.

3. What are we going to make, and how big?
The texture of the clay is vital here. If you are making small tiles, pinch-pots or small modelled forms then a smooth clay is likely to be satisfactory, but if you are intending to make forms with a thick section involving heavy modelling, or are planning large, slab-built pieces then you must use a clay which contains sand or grog (fired and ground fireclay) to assist in supporting the structure and allowing it to dry evenly. The working importance of grogged or sanded clay is dealt with in later chapters.

Hand wedging

4. Is it going to be fired?
If the work is intended for subsequent firing then the practical considerations of likely firing temperature and the thickness of the work will need to be borne in mind during the making process. There are suggestions later in the book which will help you to make more informed judgements about these questions relative to particular activities and methods.

Clay preparation

With the pressures on time and space which apply to most primary teachers it is anticipated that for most of the work which we undertake with young children, the clay can be used as it comes from the supplier, straight from the bag. Usually the clay has been de-aired and provided that the polythene bag has not been punctured (thus allowing the clay to dry), it should be ready to use. There

Fish by Matthew, aged 11. Earthenware pieces on stoneware, transparent e/w glaze.

will be times, however, when the clay is uneven and requires wedging to achieve an even consistency and remove air. This is a skill which all professional potters acquire, and is not difficult to master, although it does take a little practice. It is particularly useful when you have reclaimed some clay after a lesson and wish to even it up before storing it away. There are various methods which potters use, spiral kneading, cut and drop, and so on, but the simplest and probably most appropriate for the school situation is to work the clay as though you are kneading dough. Make sure that you do this on a wooden surface if the clay is at all sticky, and select a block of clay which you can handle comfortably. The aim is to remove all the pockets of air in the clay.

Digging and preparing your own clay

It is of course not practical for any school to dig and prepare all its clay, but there are occasions when the children bring clay into school which they have found or which has been found on school field trips. This can be a very exciting and useful discovery, and reinforce the links between the way clay is formed and local geography. It is likely that the clay will be an earthenware, and will probably contain impurities such as small stones and perhaps vegetation. The first test which you can make is to find out how plastic it is. If the clay is soft, roll it into a coil and wrap it around a finger. If it is plastic, it will do this without cracking, but if it is short the coil will snap. If you are lucky and have found some clay which you think you can use, it will need further preparation. You do this by removing as many stones and as much vegetation as possible, breaking it into small pieces, and placing it into a bucket with water to soak down. Leave it for a week or so, then mix it thoroughly and pour it through a coarse sieve. Allow it to settle again, pour off the water and dry it out to a plastic state. You then have your own school clay to test and fire. It might sound a little complicated, but it doesn't take much effort, and most time is spent drying the clay out. It is a simple process full of valuable learning for the children.

Synthetic and self-hardening clay

In recent years some pottery material suppliers have developed an air hardening clay which contains a small proportion of a non-toxic hardening agent. This has the advantage of not requiring firing to make the clay permanent, and where a kiln is not available to the school there are obvious benefits in using it. However, there are some disadvantages with this material. It tends to be rather smooth and dense, lacking the tooth and texture of clays containing sand or grog, and it is much more expensive than the natural clay. It can also harden too quickly for the work to be completed, and unlike waste clay cannot be reclaimed for re-use. Personally I like the rich, earthy smell of real clay, and if I appear biased, well perhaps I am! You might try both natural and synthetic clays and then decide for yourself.

Chapter Three
Classroom Organisation

As with all of the many aspects of learning which take place with young children, it tends to be the everyday practical issues which take time, effort and planning for success to be achieved. When we are dealing with practical subjects such as art in general, or claywork in particular, such concerns dominate the attitudes of teachers and can determine whether certain materials are used or not. There appears to be a general acceptance amongst teachers of my acquaintance that clay is an important experience for children to have, but this is tempered by worries about the mess that it could create, or with their own lack of experience in using it. This chapter will consider some of these worries and suggest strategies for overcoming them.

School organisation for claywork

If you are lucky, you may already be working in a situation where clay is used on a regular basis. There will be materials and tools available, perhaps a kiln, and a system set up for firing work and for glazing, probably with specialist knowledge at hand for advice. This naturally makes life much easier for someone planning claywork with a class for the first time. More likely, in my experience, you will find a situation where clay is used only sporadically during the year. This will be for a whole variety of reasons: because of the demands on time of other important aspects of the curriculum; of difficulty in gathering the necessary resources together, and of course, the teacher's lack of familiarity with clay. How curriculum time is managed and prioritised is a matter for the school as a whole, but developing and organising resources is a simple problem to solve. Most of the work illustrated in this book was organised from three large plastic stacking storage boxes. These were moved from room to room quite easily, and contained all the tools and bits and pieces needed to work with a whole class. (These tools are described and listed later in this chapter.) When not required they were stored away from the classroom. Once these items are collected together, you will have available resources for sharing around the school, since it is unlikely that more than one class will be using clay at any given time.

Space and group size

Unless you are in a very large school it is unlikely that you will have a specialist area to work in. You may have a wet area adjacent to the classroom which would be suitable, or perhaps some tables reserved for art and craft activities. These would allow for small group activity with say 6 to 8 children at a time. If the classroom has plastic topped tables you can deal with the lesson as a whole class activity. Most of the work in this book, with the exception of the very young children, was produced with whole classes of up to 28 children. This requires more organisation, particularly in the preparation of clay, but does avoid the distraction of other activities, or of other groups wishing they had their hands on the clay bin. It also means that the teacher can focus directly on the activity, deal quickly with issues which affect the whole group, and concentrate on practical organisation as the session proceeds. It also allows for a greater focus on the learning which is taking place and the responses by the children to their own work and that of others in the class. Shared learning and discovery are an important and valuable element in any practical activity.

We move on now to the question of what tools and equipment are appropriate for the session. This is not a prescriptive list of essentials. You can produce some wonderful work without tools at all, and many of the freshest and most lively pieces in this book came straight from the children's hands without the use of tools. Nevertheless, there are some items which are invaluable to the teacher for preparation, and for more advanced work, and these are outlined below.

Tools (see list of suppliers on page 111)

Modelling tools

These are available in both wood and plastic, and in a variety of shapes. The plastic ones are cheaper, but tend to break easily, and so I would recommend the wooden sets.

Cutting wire

This is an invaluable item, mostly used by the teacher for cutting blocks of clay to hand out, and for making slabs quickly. They do break after a while, so you will need perhaps six, between 15 inches and 18 inches long. You can make your own using stainless steel trace wire from a fishing tackle shop and wooden toggles with a small hole drilled through.

Harp

A stronger version of the cutting wire in a metal rod frame. Useful again for cutting blocks of clay and making slabs, but less flexible. Some are adjustable and allow the wire to be moved up and down to vary the thickness of the slab, but this will depend upon your supplier.

Rolling pins

These are useful for both rolling out slabs, and also for forming clay around to make cylinders. They need to be at least 1 inch thick, preferably more, and at least 12 inches long, no shorter. You can make your own using wooden broom handles or thick dowel from a timber merchant.

Tile cutters

Available from pottery suppliers, these simple tools allow square, round and hexagonal shaped tiles to be cut from slabs quickly and easily. They are useful, but limiting. You can use strong card to cut around instead. This takes a little longer, but gives more flexibility over shape and size.

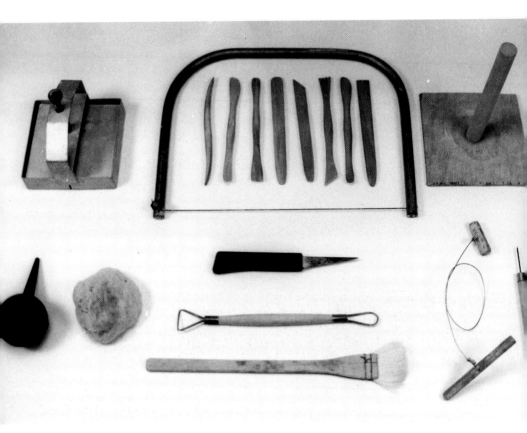

Tools

Loop tools

These are essential for hollowing out and thinning forms from the inside and they can also be used for carving into blocks of clay. They are available in different sizes and shapes, round and square-ended being the most useful, and will last for years. A selection of these will prove a valuable resource.

Brushes

You will have available bristle brushes for painting, and these are fine for use with clay slip when you are joining slabs together. However, they are not suitable for decorating with coloured slip as they are too stiff and cannot hold enough

liquid. For this work, you will need brushes with softer hair or special glaze mops from a supplier.

Sponges

Use big synthetic sponges for wiping down tables after work. A few natural sponges are also useful to smooth the work when needed. These are expensive, but last a long time if looked after and are lovely to use.

Grater

If you have not got an extruder or wad box in the school, the simple kitchen hand grater is useful for making clay hair and fur by grating the clay and removing it carefully without squeezing.

It is a bit slow, but works quite well with small groups. So does a garlic press.

Knives

You can buy potters knives, which have a thin blade and a sharp point. The thin blade is important because it doesn't stick to the clay when cutting, but there are obvious safety considerations here with young children. You might acquire a few of these, but for your use only.

Bit box

This is the 'come in handy box', which contains all those things which we collect over the years. Look out for things which will make interesting

German figures by Alex, Katie and Jack, aged 9. Slip decorated, e/w glaze.

marks and textures on clay – bits of wood and bark, old printers typeface, buttons, cogs, nuts and bolts, rope and thick string wrapped round dowel. Anything in fact which takes your or your children's fancy.

Newspaper and tape

For making simple pressmoulds.

Paper towels

For use with tiles, underneath modelled pieces when drying, and for wrapping around peg and base stands.

Equipment

Boards

You should acquire enough thin plywood modelling boards for the number of children in your class. These should be approximately 10 inches square, although the size is not that critical, and should have sanded edges to avoid splinters. They are useful in separating the work in hand from everything else on the table, and enable the work to be moved easily at the end of the session for drying. If you are planning to work with slabs you will also need some larger ply boards approximately 2 feet (61 cm) square or so, on which to stack the prepared and firmed up clay. These are also useful for moving quantities of work to the kiln.

Modelling stands, peg and base

The use of these is described later (see page 40). You will have to make them yourself or have them made locally. They consist of a piece of plywood for the base, approximately 4 inches (10 cm) square, with a length of dowel 4–5 inches (10–13 cm) long nailed on from below. It is simple, effective, and very useful for a whole variety of work.

Wad box or extruder

This is a more expensive piece of equipment, and will need to be fixed permanently to a wall or bench. It is invaluable for making quantities of coils quickly, and for extruding sections for hair or other textured decorative surfaces. This is not essential, but it is an extremely useful item for schools which use clay frequently, and/or have large groups at work.

Polythene bags and sheet

Bags are essential for wrapping spare clay and for covering work to prevent it from drying too quickly and thus cracking. Pedal bin liners are ideal and cheap. Larger polythene sheets can be used with slabs to interweave them and keep them separate, and to control drying so that they are in a good state for the children to work. If clay is tightly wrapped in polythene, it will keep for weeks in the same condition as when it was wrapped.

Canvas or hessian (burlap)

Pieces of heavy material are essential when rolling out clay to prevent it sticking to the worksurface. Around 18 inches (46 cm) square is normally quite large enough for most purposes.

Water sprayers

The hand-held sprayers used by gardeners for spraying house plants are invaluable for mist spraying both the children's work and spare clay. It keeps the clay in a moist atmosphere when wrapped in polythene, and in a warm classroom will enable the clay to be maintained in a workable state. An essential item.

Slip containers

Slip is the only liquid needed on the clay table, and then only when the children are joining leatherhard clay. Whatever container you use should have a good tight lid and a wide base to prevent it tipping over. A bowl is ideal. (For

Robot man by Ashley, aged 6. Biscuit fired.

and all manner of other forms can be suggested, and by poking in with fingers or modelling tools eyes and mouths can be formed.

For some children the association between clay and pottery is very strong, and they may well begin instinctively to hollow it out to form a simple vessel. This is not easy with a large piece of clay and tends to result in very thick walls and bases. Nevertheless this is an important and natural primitive response to the material and should not be discouraged.

Working with a lump of clay encourages a particularly sculptural approach to modelling because children have to consider the whole form at once, and begin to think about it as a fully three-dimensional object. They are obliged to explore the mass of a form and the space around it when they pull out legs and arms, etc. and these awarenesses are important elements in children's perceptual development. It is likely however that when children are faced with this experience for the first time, they will concentrate on the front of whatever they are making. This is natural because they are used to working in their drawing and painting on a flat sheet of paper. It may require some encouragement by the teacher for them to begin to realise that the back is important as well.

Carving into clay

This is a particularly sculptural method of working, involving cutting clay away from a mass to reveal a form inside, and from a conceptual viewpoint requires children to think about a subject in a subtractive way. This is not easy for many children, although the actual process is quick and direct. Using wire loop modelling tools the clay can be cut away very simply, and if mistakes are made can be just as easily replaced. If you suggest to the children that their subject is hiding inside, this will often capture their imagination and add an element of excitement to the exercise. The clay for this work needs to be grogged and open in texture because the results are likely to be quite thick in section and will crack in drying if the clay is too fine.

Modelling onto a form

This is a natural and instinctive process for most children. By applying pellets, coils and flat pieces of clay, a form can be very quickly animated and enriched, and this process probably more than any other results in the characteristic vigour and vitality of children's work. There are problems however which both the children and teacher need to be aware of. Firstly, simply pushing moist clay onto a form does not produce a secure join. The moisture in the clay will hold the two pieces together at the time, but when they dry, the added section will invariably fall off. It is very important that children are taught from an early stage to rub in the join with their fingers or a modelling tool to ensure that there is a sound and secure bond.

Secondly, because clay can be rolled out into long coils or strips, children will tend to extend their forms outwards with arms, legs, tails and so on. Whilst the clay is plastic, there is no problem to this provided again that there is a secure join, but when the model dries these extensions become extremely fragile and tend to break when being handled.

Monster by Daniel, aged 6. Biscuit fired.

Modelling over a bottle

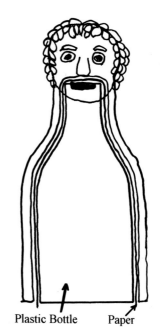

Plastic Bottle   Paper

Peg and base animal

Peg and base puppet

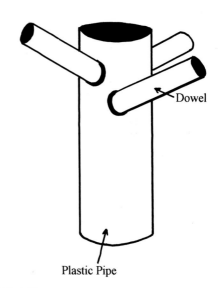

Dowel

Plastic Pipe

Modelling a tree

The teacher therefore must strike a careful balance between encouraging the children to explore freely, and making the children aware of the limitations of clay when it dries. This naturally will come with experience, but it is a shame when a batch of work falls apart due to a lack of care with joining. It is sometimes worthwhile at the end of a session for the teacher to quietly check the joins at the early stages to minimise losses.

Supports for modelling

For much of the work which children model there is no need for additional support, particularly when working with a fairly compact block of clay. However, if they begin to pinch out the legs of an animal for example, the weight of the body will squash them down, and unless the model is left upside down to dry far

39

enough to support the weight there will be problems.

The Peg and Base which has been described earlier under Tools is extremely useful in this situation, allowing the model to be supported from underneath whilst the legs and other details are completed. When it is finished, the model can be removed to check that the legs are the same length by placing it gently

onto a surface, and then returning it onto the stand to dry.

Puppet heads can be modelled on these stands from a solid lump of clay, provided the base is wide enough to keep the clay stable. The peg is useful for these because a longer neck can be made to allow for attaching a fabric sleeve later.

Taller forms such as figures can also be supported using this method. The peg must first be wrapped with a few layers of paper to provide a good release between the clay and peg, and then the clay can be pushed on to form the body. The rest of the work can then be completed with little risk of the model collapsing. Once it is completed, the model must be removed quickly from the peg. This is important, because if the clay dries and shrinks it can be very difficult to pull off. The paper can remain inside the model, as it will just burn away during the firing.

Left
Halloween sprite by Scott, aged 4. Biscuit fired.

Anteater by Tom, aged 6. Biscuit fired.

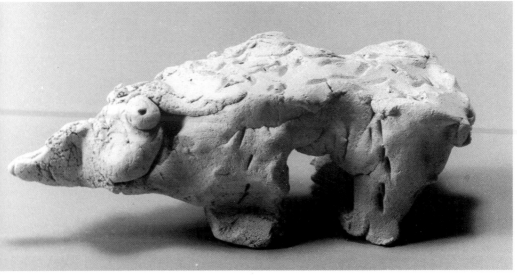

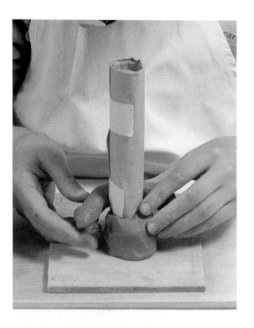

Beginning to add coils around a paper-covered peg.

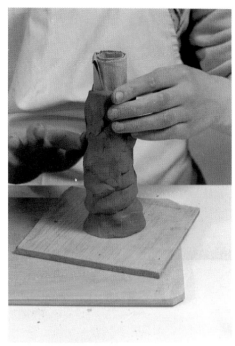

Building the body.

Adding coils for arms.

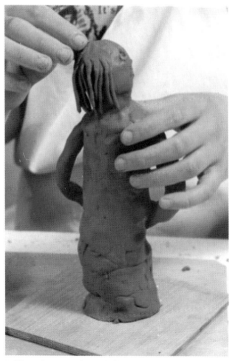

Adding hair and modelling details.

These are just two examples of ways in which this support may be used. You may well develop others to suit your particular work, but it is an extremely useful way of encouraging very young children to work on a larger scale, and with relative ease. Plastic bottles of different sizes can also be used in a similar way to provide wider forms, and methods of using all of these with slabs are described in Chapter Six.

There may be occasions when a very much bigger support is required for a particular subject or group work. This obviously will require preparation by the teacher and will vary according to what is being planned, but whatever you decide you must consider how the support will be removed once the modelling is finished. One example of a piece which was made in this way is the large tree with the owl and birds made with a group of 4–5 year old children (p.14). A plastic pipe was used as a main support, with holes cut to allow fat dowels to be pushed in for the branches.

Terracotta statues, Cyprus, 6th–5th century BC. *Courtesy of the Ashmolean Museum.*

Two ladies with a scarf and necklace by Amy, aged 4 and Natalie, aged 5.

(You could use a strong wide cardboard tube instead.) The whole support was then covered with a few layers of newspaper which were held in place with tape. The children then covered the support, as a group, with a good layer of grogged clay to a thickness of approximately ½ inch (12 mm), marking and texturing the surface. They then modelled the birds individually and joined them on to the branches. When it was completed the piece was allowed to dry for an hour or so, then the dowels were pulled out, and the central support removed. The whole activity took around an hour for each group, which was appropriate given their span of concentration.

Modelling a head on a peg.

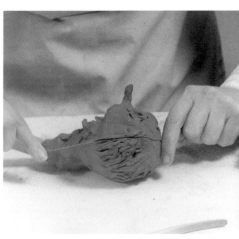

Cutting the piece in half with a wire.

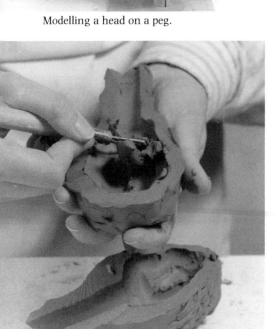

Hollowing out a core with a loop tool.

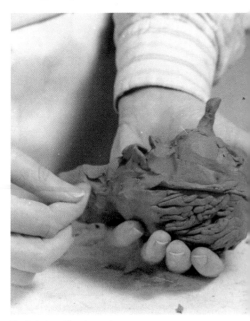

Re-joining the two pieces.

Hollowing modelled work for firing

If the end results are to be fired, and the clay thickness is greater than $\frac{1}{2}$ inch (12 mm), it is essential to thin out the forms to prevent them blowing up in the kiln.

Simple forms can often be hollowed out quickly and easily from the bottom using a wire loop tool. However, there are some pieces, such as solid puppet heads for example, where this is not possible because of a narrow neck. In this case, you will need to cut the model open carefully with a wire, hollow out the two halves, and then carefully rejoin the pieces. Remember to ensure that if air is trapped inside, there is a small air hole to prevent cracking during drying and firing.

Another method which is useful when you have thicker sections in a piece, and where hollowing out is impractical, is to push a thin dowel or paintbrush handle up into the clay. This makes a small hole which will assist in allowing moisture to escape during the firing.

Pinching

Unlike working from a lump of clay, the process of pinching requires direction from the teacher at the outset, because there are specific skills involved, which need to be demonstrated.

Method

1. Take a piece of clay that is of a size that can be comfortably held in the palm of the hand. This will naturally vary with the age of the child.
2. Roll it into a ball between the hands. This may be difficult with some very young children and require a little practice.
3. Holding the ball in the palm of one hand, gently push the thumb of the other hand into the centre to form a hollow. You may need to stress **not** to push the thumb right through or you will have to start again! Again very young children may need help with this with their small wiggly thumbs.
4. Still holding the clay in one hand,

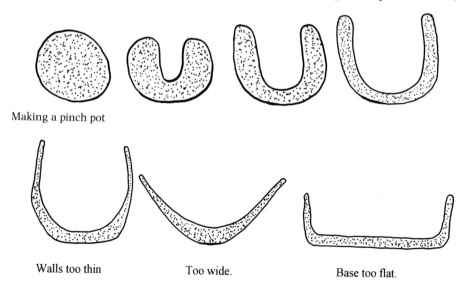

Making a pinch pot

Walls too thin   Too wide.   Base too flat.

Problems with pinch pots

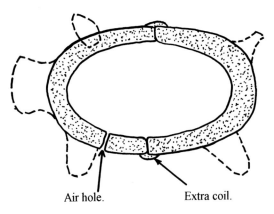

Air hole.   Extra coil.

Joining two pinch pots

There are three common problems with this process, easy though it may seem to an adult. Firstly, if the children pinch too vigorously the form tends to spread out, resulting in a wide floppy form. Secondly, if they pinch unevenly they may leave the clay thick at the bottom and thin at the top. Thirdly, if they carelessly drop the pot on the table, or try to pinch it out without holding it in the palm of the hand, the base will level out, resulting in an ashtray form. The teacher needs to be aware of these potential problems whilst the children are working.

Once mastered, this simple process provides a basic form that can be used in a variety of ways, for example by joining two bowls to make a hollow form, or by further adding coils, which will be discussed in Chapter Five.

and preferably with the thumb on the inside, the children should gently squeeze the wall upwards. After each squeeze the pot should be turned a little, developing a rhythmic process of turning and squeezing. This takes practice to master, but the aim should be to produce a small bowl with an even section, not too thick at the bottom, nor too thin on the rim.

Pig. Roman, 1st–2nd century AD. *Courtesy of the Ashmolean Museum.*

Thinning the walls of a pinch pot.

Adding prickles to a hedgehog made from two joined pinch pots.

Joining pinched forms

Once the children can make simple pinch pots with a degree of consistency, they can move on to join two of them together. This is a straightforward process as follows.

1. Use two pinch pots of the same diameter and with a rim thickness of at least $\frac{1}{4}$ inch (6 mm).
2. Moisten the rims with a damp sponge.
3. Gently push the two pots together and rub over the joint with a dry finger to make a secure join. If there is a hollow at the join, a small roll of clay can be added onto the outside

and modelled in. The air trapped inside will help to retain the form whilst it is worked on further. It is essential that a small air hole be made at the end of the session to allow the trapped air to escape when the clay shrinks during drying, and also to prevent it blowing apart during firing.

From these simple rounded forms children can develop all manner of subjects by modelling on other features to create owls, pigs, mice, hedgehogs, rabbits or whatever their imagination suggests. The pinch pot is also a good starting point for subsequent work with coils as described in the next chapter.

Terracotta cow. Roman, 1st–2nd century AD, Italy. *Courtesy of the Ashmolean Museum.*

Chapter Five
Building with Coils

A long tradition

The process of making vessels using coils or strips of clay is one which is common to all cultures from the dawn of civilisation. In many countries it is still the principal method by which pots are made for daily use. The invention of the potters wheel subsequently enabled clay to be worked much faster and allowed for the development of a wider variety of forms, but it is the coil-built form which provides the common ground in work from traditional societies.

The individual characteristics of these pots naturally vary according to the societies which produced them. South American work is often richly decorated

Cremation urns, Anglo Saxon, from Lackford, England, *c.* AD1570. *Courtesy of the Ashmolean Museum.*

with crisp geometric patterns, fish and faces; African pots are often enriched with surface texture and patterning by impressing and modelling onto the surface. Early Japanese Jomon ware has very strong surface modelling with a vigorous handling of the clay, thereby giving a particularly robust quality to the work.

All these pieces have the same common practical purposes in that they were used for storing – food, grain, seeds, clothes, liquids, water, beer etc., and they were also often used over an open fire for cooking. The rounded forms which they all have as a common feature are derived not just from the fact that they were all made in a similar fashion, which of course they were, but from the practical discovery that a rounded form is much less prone to cracking when heated over a fire. The

stresses which are created by heat are more easily spread when the form has a rounded base, and this factor is also important during the firing.

Most of this work has been fired in a simple clamp or brushwood bonfire to a relatively low temperature, approximately 700°–900°C. The pots remain quite fragile at this temperature, and also porous. This is useful in hot countries, because liquids will evaporate through the walls, and help to keep the contents cool.

It is outside the framework of this book to deal in more detail with this wonderful historical source for work in school, but it is important that children gain some understanding of the relationships between their simple coil pots and the pots produced over the centuries by their own and other cultures.

The making of a simple vessel is a basic and instinctive reaction to clay. The idea of making a container to put something into seems to fulfil an important human need. For children this is a special experience, and whatever else they do with clay it is something not to be missed.

There are three methods by which coils can be made – by hand, with a tool, and with an extruder.

Making coils by hand

This might seem to be a very easy process, and in many ways it is, but like many apparently simple skills it requires some practice to achieve consistently even coils of clay. Children will need to be taught these skills, and it is a good idea for the teacher to practise them beforehand to develop an understanding of the problems which might be encountered during the session. The following points are suggested as a guide when developing this work with the children.

1. The clay should be soft to begin with, but not sticky. If it is at all dry, the coils will crack.
2. Give yourself plenty of room on the table and put the modelling boards to one side as they restrict arm movement.
3. Take a piece of clay about the size of a small apple and squeeze it into an even sausage shape.
4. Then begin to roll it gently backwards and forwards across the table. The important thing to stress to the children is to use the **whole** hand, from the tips of the fingers to the wrist, and **not** to press too hard. It requires only a gentle pressure or the coils will flatten out.
5. If this happens, a change of speed with very gentle pressure will often bring the coils back to a round shape again. You might need to help the children with this initially.
6. When the children first begin this exercise, there will always be some individuals who will try to make the coils as long as possible. The longer the coils are, the more difficult they are to control as the children will quickly find out, but it is great fun to begin with!
   A length of around 12 inches (30 cm) is ideal, although very young children will need to work with less.
7. Encourage the children to move their hands sideways to achieve an even coil. It is a good idea to have a piece of dowel or a fibre pen as an example of the thickness which they should be aiming for. Very thin coils should be avoided as they tend to break when used.

Coil pot by Laura, aged 6. Light brown e/w glaze, fired to 1140°C.

Coil pot by Sarah, aged 6. Smoke-fired.

8. Have the children build up a small stack of coils before they begin to construct their work so that they do not have to move their work to one side every few minutes to make more coils.

With a little practice and instruction the children will soon master this skill, and once learnt it will be used readily, not just for constructing objects, but for all sorts of decorative applications.

Making coils with tools

A quick method of making coils is to use a wire loop tool. By pulling it through a block of clay as near to the surface as possible a large number of coils can be produced quite quickly. However, because the clay particles have not been aligned as happens when rolling by hand, there is a tendency for coils produced in this way to break rather easily. Also, remember that the size of the coil will be determined by the diameter of the wire loop. Nevertheless, this is a useful technique if you wish to make coils for decoration.

Making coils using an extruder

There are a number of simple extruders (sometimes called a wad box) on the market. These are available from pottery suppliers. Unless a school has a designated area for claywork, this equipment is probably inappropriate, because it needs to be fixed permanently to a wall or bench and will take up valuable space. However, they have a place in larger schools, and by changing dies it is possible to produce fairly speedily a variety of sections, including round and square tubes, which could well be useful forms for some projects.

Making coils with a loop

Making coils with an extruder.

Older children should be able to use these extruders themselves once they have been shown how they work.

Building forms with coils

The potential for producing a wide variety of forms with coils is immense, and once the basics have been mastered children will use this process to develop their ideas into figures, animals and a whole variety of imaginative creatures. However, since the first work with coils usually centres around the making of a simple pot, here is the process and some of the common problems.

Making a simple vessel

1. Start with clay that is soft, but not sticky, and make a stack of coils as previously described. (If you have an extruder, it can be useful with young children and large groups to prepare a good quantity of coils before the session.)
2. Either take a ball of clay and flatten it out to make a base, or using a coil, make a spiral of the required size. Make sure that you have a layer of paper between the clay and the modelling board to prevent the clay from sticking. If you used coils for the base, smooth over the joins with fingers or a modelling tool.
3. The walls of the pot can now be started by adding coils one by one and breaking them off to length, or by spiralling up with one length. It is important that no more than three widths are added at a time, and for beginners, just one. This will help to control the shape of the pot, and ensure that each join is carefully smoothed over. If this is not done, they will separate when they dry.
4. Joining is best done by smoothing **downwards** with the fingers or a tool, trying to avoid pinching the wall, and supporting the wall on the outside with the hand when smoothing inside. Children love squeezing clay, but if they squeeze the coils, the wall will become too thin to build onto. If the pot is to have the coils left as a decorative outside, then just smooth the inside, but it **must** be done thoroughly.
5. If the pot is built out of single coils, avoid having the end joins one above the other.
6. The shape of the pot will be determined by the way in which the coils are placed onto each other. There is a tendency for beginners to place the coils either on top or just to the outside, and they very quickly find that their pot has spread out into a bowl and has become floppy

and unmanageable. In this situation they may have to start again. Alternatively, the teacher, by cutting a V shape out of the wall and rejoining the coils, can help to correct the problem.

7. There is a limit to how high a pot can be built without it sagging at the base from the weight. If this starts to happen, the pot must be allowed to firm up for a while, but the top must be kept moist with a layer of damp cloth or paper.

8. Closing in the walls is achieved by placing coils just to the **inside** of the wall and smoothing them over from the outside.

9. If the classroom is warm, and the clay has been handled a great deal, cracks may begin to appear in the coils towards the end of the session. A damp sponge will help to smooth these over if they appear, and covering the stock of coils with damp paper or polythene from the start will help to minimise the problem.

10. In my experience, you should resist the temptation to have water on the table when making coil pots. It is much easier to join the coils if fingers are dry and the clay is not sticky.

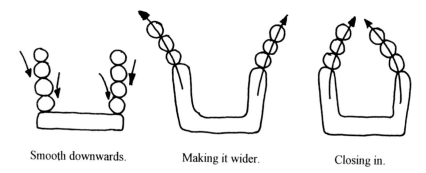

Smooth downwards.   Making it wider.   Closing in.

Building a coil pot

Cut a V in the wall.

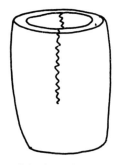

Join the wall firmly.

Correcting a wide form

Figure of an owl, decorated with underglaze colours, 19th century. *Courtesy of the Hanley Museum, Stoke on Trent.*

Developing coil-built forms

Besides using coils to make pots of various kinds, the skill of coiling, once learned, can be used to produce forms which can be turned into a whole range of subjects. This development will require an understanding by the children of the state of the clay, and an awareness of how the form will support itself whilst it is being worked. If the clay is soft, there are likely to be problems with certain forms until the clay has reached a leatherhard state, particularly those which are wide and round. If the walls are closed up, making a roughly spherical form, the air trapped inside can be used to provide some strength,

although even with this, care will still be needed.

Suggestions for possible subjects using a rounded coil form include animals such as pigs, hedgehogs, guinea pigs, rabbits, mice, elephants, and hippos. Other subjects could include birds, which generally have a nice rounded body form, and some fish also could be considered, particularly if the body is flattened a little. Taller subjects made from an elongated vessel could include squirrels and weasels, or some birds with a compact upright stance, such as owls.

Whatever subject is chosen there are certain important practical and visual considerations. Firstly, it is essential that the children are given first-hand or good second-hand visual material to look at. They need to be aware of the overall form of the subject, and be aware of the surface quality and patterning of feathers, fur or scales before they begin. Secondly, there needs to be a consideration of what clay can and cannot allow in representing some subjects. Birds, for example, will need a base of some sort to support the body, or be shown in a squatting position because you cannot support a heavy body on fine clay legs. Similarly, any animals will need to have legs attached at the end of the process, and then be left on their sides to firm up if they are not to collapse. It is useful to have some pieces of sheet sponge available for this work to provide a soft cushion to rest the models on.

Whatever you are making, remember that the children will use any method at their disposal to realise their ideas, and that once they understand how to make coils, or slabs of clay, they will happily combine them with modelling in a whole variety of ways.

Finally, as mentioned in the previous chapter, make sure that a small hole is made underneath any form which has been enclosed to allow the air to escape during drying and firing.

Fish by the Martin Brothers, stoneware, *c.* 1900. *Courtesy of the Hanley Museum, Stoke on Trent.*

Decorating with coils

Once children have developed the ability to make coils, and this can happen very quickly with even young children, they will instinctively begin to use them for both decoration and modelling. They will also break pieces off to make small round pellets with their fingers. It is important if soft coils are being added to a leatherhard pot that a little slip (see Working Methods, Chapter 3) is brushed on to help make the join. This also applies to modelling coils and pellets onto tiles. In fact, any time that you are joining soft clay to a drier and harder clay, a little slip is advisable. Use a small brush and encourage the children to be sparing in the way they apply it, or you could end up with a messy surface. One final problem which can occur with coils is the way children use them to make tails, arms and long ears. Try to ensure that very long, thin extensions of clay are joined to the main mass of the form along as much of the length as possible. The children don't realise at first that the

Dancer, Chinese, Tang Dynasty, 8th century AD. *Courtesy of the Ashmolean Museum.*

clay will dry out and become very brittle, and it is almost impossible to get a very thin and long form through the kiln without breaking it. Snakes can be a kiln packer's nightmare!

Left
'My Rabit' by Ryan, aged 6.

Chapter Six
Working with Slabs of Clay

Slabwork can be approached in a variety of ways, and at a number of levels, depending upon the ability and experience of the children. These can range from small tiles to larger constructions such as houses and figures. Naturally, the larger and more complicated the work, the greater the technical demands become, but all the methods outlined in this chapter are within the ability of primary children. The teacher will need to use his/her judgement as to what is appropriate for a particular project.

There are three ways of making slabs: cutting, rolling by hand, and using a slab roller. The later is an expensive piece of equipment and not likely to be available in a primary school, but the first two methods are simple and fairly easy to master.

Making slabs by cutting

This is by far the simplest and quickest method of producing flat pieces of clay, and it is ideal for small pieces. It is a particularly recommended method for use by teachers of very young children who may have difficulty in rolling clay themselves, and where the preparation for the lesson needs to be carried out beforehand by the teacher. There are two disadvantages, however, in using this process. Firstly, if the clay contains grog or sand the surface will be rough after cutting and this may not be

required, and secondly, because the clay has not been rolled it may contain air bubbles and lack strength. The latter can be overcome by wedging, but if the children are simply working on flat tile surfaces, it should not be a problem. Small air bubbles which appear can be pricked with a needle and pressed down. The clay for slabmaking needs to be slightly firmer than for other methods, and it is especially important that it is not sticky. If it is too soft, allow it to stand out well before the session to firm up.

1. Form the clay into a block slightly larger than the slab size which you need, by gently dropping and turning it onto the table.
2. Place the block onto a hessian-covered board and place wooden guides on either side. The thickness of these will determine how thick the slab itself will be.
3. Using a cutting wire held taut onto the top of the guides, cut through the clay towards you, and remove the block. Place the slab onto a piece of polythene sheet or a paper towel and repeat the process.
4. A harp can be used in a similar fashion, and of course does not need wooden guides.
5. Build up a store of slabs with a layer of polythene or paper between each one to prevent them sticking together. It is useful to make more than are

Making slabs by cutting with a wire and guides.

Making slabs using a harp.

needed for a session to avoid having to break off during the activity. If polythene is used between the slabs, they can be tightly wrapped and will keep for a number of days, which makes the lesson organisation much easier.

Making slabs by rolling

This is a more complicated method in that it requires more control of the clay and greater manual dexterity. However, children with previous experience of clay should manage the process with instruction and, as will be explained,

there are ways of overcoming some problems. You will need:

a. Hessian-covered boards, or pieces of canvas.
b. 2 wooden strips for each child to act as thickness guides.
c. Rolling pins or thick wooden dowels of a suitable length.

1. As before make sure that your clay is not sticky.
2. Take a lump of clay, place it on a board and flatten it out with the hands to a thickness of approximately 1 inch ($2\frac{1}{2}$ cm). It is essential that you cover the board with hessian or fabric, because if you roll the clay out on a plastic table it will stick completely. Turn the block over and press from the other side.
3. Place the guides on either side of the clay with enough space to allow the clay to spread, and using the rolling pin, roll the clay out. It is important that the rolling pin is long enough to cover both the width of the clay and the guides, and the children may need to be reminded in their enthusiasm that the guides are there for a purpose! The children will need to be standing up for this work in order to get enough pressure in the rolling pin.
4. Don't try to roll the clay out in one go. It is essential to turn the clay over to release it from the cloth. The children may need to be shown that it is easier to turn the clay over and peel the canvas from the back, particularly if the clay is thin. If they try to pull it up from the top, it is likely to tear.
5. When the slab has been rolled to the correct thickness, place it on a modelling board with a paper towel underneath, ready for working.

Flattening out the clay before rolling.

Rolling out, using hessian and wooden guide strips.

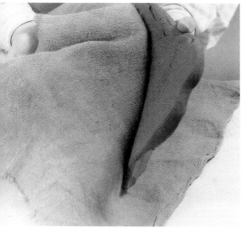

Peeling the hessian from the back of the clay.

Children initially can have problems in using the wooden guides, and if you are planning to use this method, particularly with very young children, it may help if you make some boards with the guides nailed to the edges, and use a heavy paper underneath the clay. This will help to ensure that the rolling pin remains on the guides and that the clay has an even thickness.

Making tiles

Either of the methods described above will result in the flat surface needed for tiles, but this is just the start. There are a number of practical problems which teachers need to be aware of when making tiles with their children, and which can make the difference between success and failure.

1. Give thought to the clay you are using. Ideally, the clay should contain some sand or grog which will allow a thicker section (between $\frac{3}{8}$–$\frac{1}{2}$ inch, or 8–12 mm) to be worked. This will allow the children to exploit the natural texture of the clay. The thickness can be controlled by the height of the guides used.
2. If you only have a smooth dense clay available, it is advisable to make the tile thinner, say $\frac{1}{4}$–$\frac{1}{2}$ inch (5–8 mm), and not to have a finished surface larger than 6 inches (15 cm), preferably smaller. This will help to prevent cracking and warping during drying.
3. Make sure that there is a layer of polythene, or preferably paper, underneath the tile so that when the children press the surface it does not stick.
4. Give thought to the ways in which

you want the children to work the surface. If they are building up texture by adding on coils and shapes, provided they don't make the tile too thick, the results should be satisfactory. If they are drawing or cutting into the surface with a stick or a modelling tool, or impressing a deep design, however, there can be very real problems. This is because when the clay is moist, the tile appears to be in one piece, but as it dries and needs to be handled, it breaks into small pieces, which is a real disappointment. This can be a particular difficulty with very thin tiles, and I suggest that drawing in thin clay be avoided if the work is to be kept.

5. Think about the shape of the tile. We adults often tend to think of tiles as having a rectangular or square shape, but for children, particularly young ones, the shape is often of little importance. For them, marking, drawing, impressing and building up an image is the most important experience and is part of the delight in working the material.

6. Making square, rectangular or other geometric shapes is straightforward, and can be an excellent group activity linking well with other curriculum areas, notably mathematics. If the intention is to produce a panel from a group project, some planning is

Henry VIII by Craig, aged 10, Stoneware fired to 1260°C, with iron oxide rubbed into the surface details.

obviously needed if the tiles are to fit together. Simple thick card templates can be used at the start to give the basic shape, and the children can then carry on. There is little point in spending much time at the beginning cutting an exact shape, because as soon as the children start working the tile it will spread out. Once they have finished, and preferably when the tile has become leatherhard, the card template can be used to trim the edges accurately.

7. Some pottery suppliers market simple tile cutters in different shapes. These have their uses, but a card template gives much more flexibility over the design.

8. The real problem with tiles comes in the drying stage. It is here that a more open, grogged clay is an advantage. If the tiles are left out to dry on a board, the top surface dries more quickly and they curl up at the edges. Sometimes this can lead to quite large cracks developing. The secret is to slow the drying down by placing the tiles onto corrugated card or something similar, covering them with polythene, and turning them over once or twice to allow both sides to dry evenly.

This then is an introduction to making slabs and working them in a very simple way. A great deal of very exciting work can be produced just using flat clay surfaces, and of course children are familiar with working on a flat surface from all their other daily activities.

We now move onto forming with slabs, and whilst some of these methods are more complicated and demanding for the children, many can be used with infants. The teacher will need to consider carefully the ability of the class, and in

Making tiles with a tile cutter.

Using a card template to make different shaped tiles.

the case of some processes, prepare the slabs beforehand to maximise the time for the creative activity of the children. This is a fine judgement, but one which all primary teachers are aware of, and the results are well worth the effort.

Forming by drape and pressmoulding

This involves either shaping the slab over a simple mould or pressing it into a hollow former. Traditionally, potters used biscuit or plaster moulds to make rectangular or square dishes for their production ware, and there are many examples of these in our museums. Sometimes they would press the clay into two halves of a mould and join them to make square bottles and vases. For our purposes, it is unlikely that enough moulds will be available in the average primary classroom, but there are some very simple ways of drape and pressmoulding which can be used with smaller groups.

The important practical element in this work is to find a way to support the rather floppy slab of clay whilst it is being worked upon, and to also support it whilst it is drying.

Draping

First, you have to find or make the mould to support the clay. The shape of the mould is important if it is made from something hard. When clay dries, it shrinks tight onto the mould and cannot be removed easily. There is also the

Draping a clay slab over a newspaper former.

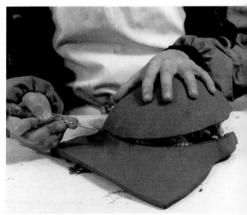

Cutting away the excess clay.

Modelling on details.

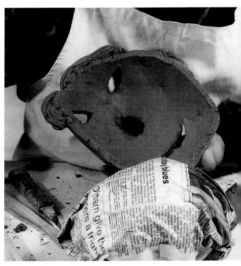

Lifting the model off the former to hollow out the nose from behind.

likelihood of it splitting. A shallow mould is therefore much better because the form lifts away easily as it contracts. If you look around, you will realise that there are many forms which we use in the home which can be used for drape moulds. If you use a hard mould, it is essential that a barrier, usually two or three layers of newsprint held in place with tape, be placed between the clay and the surface to prevent the clay from sticking.

A simple method of making drape moulds for groups of children is to use newspaper crumpled up into large balls and wrapped with full sheets. This allows for a variety of shapes, which can be long or round, large or small, depending upon what is needed. Once enough paper has been used to make a **firm** mould shape, it can be taped together lightly to hold the edges. Such paper moulds are cheap and quick to produce, and have the advantage that they shrink a little when the clay dries, and so the work can be left on them at the end of the session. They are ideal for making masks, faces and tortoises etc.

It is useful to separate the work lightly from the paper mould before they dry too far, because sometimes the children wrap the slab round underneath, preventing release. This release from the mould is also important if the children have built up thick modelling onto the surface of the slab, for example, a big nose. By removing the paper, the clay can be thinned out from the back with a modelling tool or wire loop to retain an even thickness, before being replaced on the mould to dry.

Pressmoulding

This involves placing the slab into a mould to produce a dish or bowl form.

The mould will then support the clay whilst it is being worked on, and also whilst it dries. As with drape moulding, the better moulds are again shallow, because a deep mould is difficult to fill with the clay without it tearing.

The mould itself can be made from almost anything, as long as it is strong enough to take the weight of the clay and the pressure of working. It is similarly important to ensure that there is a barrier of thin paper or polythene

Pressing clay into a bowl mould.

Trimming excess clay from the edge.

between the clay and the mould to allow easy release, although there is less of a problem when pressmoulding because the clay shrinks inwards, and naturally assists a release.

Further development using pressmoulding and drape moulding

The problem with all moulds is that the form of the mould tends to dictate the form of the clay. However, there are ways of using moulds which allow more flexibility over the final form of the piece. For example, you can use two moulds, fill them both, and join them when the clay is firm enough to keep its shape, thereby making a larger hollow form. This is a way of making bigger spherical or ovoid forms, and is very much quicker than coiling. Equally, you can use the drape method over a rounded ball of paper, and by placing two slabs on either side, and then joining them at the edge a spherical form can be produced which is supported from the inside. This is a safer method than pressmoulding two halves

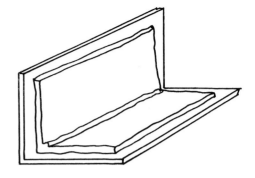

Using angled boards

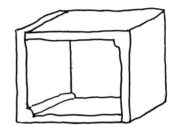

Joining to make a box

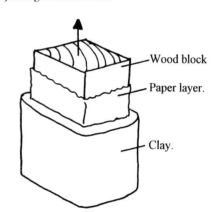

Wood block

Paper layer.

Clay.

Wood block former

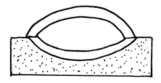

Joining two pressmoulds

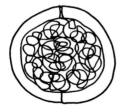

Using a paper former

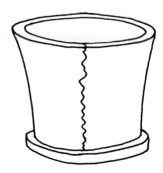

Making a Tyg

together where the support is lacking. Remember to make a hole in the sphere to allow the air to escape during drying and firing. If the piece is not too large, the paper can be left in to burn away during the firing or, alternatively, leave a large enough hole in the base to pull out the paper when the clay is leatherhard.

The moulds which have been suggested so far have been round, but there is no reason why you cannot use angled moulds. Two pieces of wooden board joined at an angle will give two sides of a box form which could be used as the starting point for a building, or the sides of a square vase. You can also use blocks of wood covered in clay to make small houses forms. The wood blocks must be covered with several layers of paper and a film of polythene before you begin, and the block must be removed immediately the work is finished or it will crack the clay in drying.

Balloons can also be used as moulds, giving a round form which is a good support for modelling a large head. The balloon needs to stand in a bowl or flowerpot to prevent it rolling around whilst the clay is being applied, but once this has been done the children can model on it quite freely. At the end, when the clay has stiffened they can pop the balloon and pull it out from the base. For obvious reasons, don't let them use sharp tools to model with!

Building with flat slabs

This is a more advanced and demanding method of construction, which requires careful planning, an understanding of the condition of the clay, and some skills in joining the slabs together. It is a superb design exercise for older children, involving measuring sides, thinking

a. Fix legs to base. b. Make a cylinder for the body and join well to legs inside. c. Close top and add head. d. Finish modelling and use a stick to ensure no air is trapped.

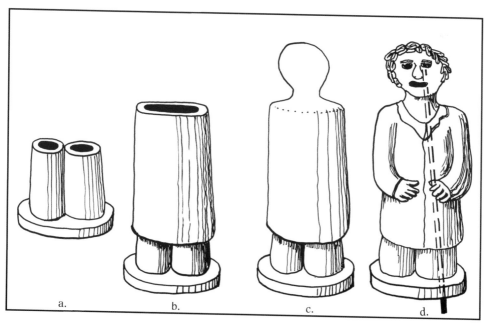

a.   b.   c.   d.

Medieval Tyg, earthenware with sprig decoration, 1635. *Courtesy of the Ashmolean Museum.*

Below
Henry VIII and Catherine of Aragon mugs by Gregory and Oliver, aged 10. Made with slabs joined to a base, then modelled and slip decorated, earthenware glaze, fired to 1060°C.

about joins and allowing for the thickness of the clay, and also, if you are making houses, how the roof will fit to the walls.

The method naturally lends itself to forms such as houses and boxes, and with care can result in quite large structures. You should also consider other forms which could be made using this principle. For example, the Tygs and Face Mugs were made by forming a cylinder of clay, joining the edge, and then attaching this to a base. Other forms which are more asymmetrical could also be considered, as, for example, the vessels based on the work of Alison Britton, made by 10–11 year old children (page 104).

Making a small box form

1. Roll out a slab of clay to the thickness you require. For a small box around 6 inches (15 cm) square, a thickness of $\frac{1}{4}$ inch (6 mm) minimum will be satisfactory, thicker for larger

structures. Work out how much you will need for the base, sides and top.

2. Allow the clay to stiffen up to a firm leatherhard state. This is **very** important, because if you try to build with floppy clay you will have a problem keeping the shape.

3. Cut out the base and two opposite sides. Cut out the two ends which will be narrower because of the thickness of the clay. This is a nice little design problem for the children, which if you approach it by questioning will get them thinking about the problems of simple constructions.

4. A good sequence for constructing the box is to join two sides at right angles, then join these to the base. This provides some support and strength

Two bombed houses by Jack, aged 10 and Craig, aged 9. Slip decorated stoneware clay, matt earthenware glaze, fired to 1140°C. Based on a World War II project.

for joining the remaining two sides.

5. Before you begin to construct, score around the edges of the base, and the edges to be joined on the sides.

6. Paint the joins with a thin layer of clay slip as you go, and press the edges together. Crosshatching with a needle along the joint will help to blend the two surfaces. Smooth the join inside and out with a modelling tool, supporting it with the hand, and making sure that you have a good bond.

7. Finally, make some thin coils of clay

Stages in making a slab box. Marking out the clay.

Scoring the edges to be joined.

Painting slip on the joins.

Adding a coil of clay inside to strengthen the join.

Scratching and smoothing the joints.

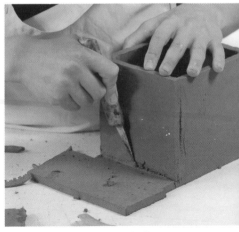

Cutting excess clay from the base.

and use them on the inside of the join as an added reinforcement.

8. If you are adding a lid, this can be given a rim by adding a roll of clay underneath to locate it on the base.

Making larger slab constructions such as houses

The same principles of making apply to large forms as to the small box just described. However, the larger your work, the more important some aspects become. The clay must be leatherhard and able to support its own weight without distortion. Joins must also be particularly well made, with great care taken over modelling the joint, and reinforcing it on the inside. If you have a large base, it is essential that there are some layers of paper underneath to allow the piece to shrink across the board. This is not a process for children who are unfamiliar with clay. I would suggest that you use it with older

Model of a house, Chinese, Han Dynasty, AD618–906. *Courtesy of the Ashmolean Museum.*

Christening cradle, English, 18th or 19th century. *Courtesy of the Ashmolean Museum.*

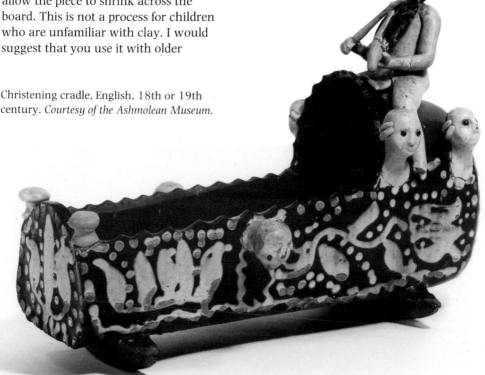

Standing bird, earthenware pieces on stoneware, white semi opaque earthenware glaze, 1140°C.

'Mabel the cleaner' by Rebecca, aged 10.

children who have greater hand eye coordination, and who understand about leatherhard clay. If the joins are not made carefully, there is a real danger of cracks appearing either during drying or at the firing stage. This is particularly likely if the clay has been allowed to dry too much before assembling the form. Spraying the clay with a mist of water, wrapping it in damp cloth, and when it is finished wrapping it in polythene to even out and dry slowly will all help to minimise the risk.

Decorating the surface

This will be dealt with in more detail in the next chapter, but it is worth pointing out here that if you require the children to decorate the surface of their slab form by impressing or adding on, it is better to do as much of this as possible whilst the clay is flat, and before they cut the shapes out to assemble them. Trying to impress a completed box will inevitably distort the form and strain the edges.

The bombed houses were made by children aged 9–11 as part of a topic on the Second World War. They had no previous experience of working with slabs of clay in this way, and once the basic methods had been explained, were quite able to carry on and solve any problems on the way. The boys were really enthusiastic about making the bombed and derelict houses, whilst the girls were equally concerned that their houses were intact and supplied with chimneys and chimney pots! A medium grogged stoneware clay was used for these, painted with coloured slips, and fired with a semi-matt earthenware glaze.

Using supports with slabs

For some forms a simple support can be very useful, and enable the children to work softer clay slabs with ease. The peg and base described earlier is one such support, but there are many others which you can improvise depending on what you are making. I have used plastic bottles as supports for making figures with 4–5 year old children, and they have been extremely successful.

The fish and bird (pp. 26 and 70) were made using a peg and base. Paper was first wrapped around the peg, and then two basic shapes were cut out from stoneware slabs, placed either side of the peg, and the edges squeezed together and firmly joined. In these examples the scales and feathers were added using an earthenware clay to provide both rich surface texture and colour. (See Chapter Seven, Using different clays together.) The fins and wings were then modelled onto the basic form. All these pieces were allowed to dry on the support after first checking that there was plenty of room around the peg to allow for shrinkage, and that the bases were level so that they would stand when they were taken off. Plastic bottles can be used in the same way (see page 39). They allow for fatter and taller forms. However, it is particularly important with these that there are several layers of paper around the bottle to prevent sticking, and that the paper is not wrapped too tightly. In addition, you **must** remove the bottle as soon as the children have finished working. If there is any delay and the clay shrinks it can be extremely difficult to pull out the support. The principle advantage of using these supports is that the work cannot collapse whilst the children are working the clay. How much initial preparation you carry out as the teacher will depend entirely on the ability of your children.

With very young children you will need to wrap the support and prepare the slabs in advance as described earlier. You might even wrap the slab around the support to give them a start, but this is a decision which needs to be taken in relation to the learning which you wish them to experience. Older children will have little problem with this once they have been shown the basic method.

Figures made with slabs

A direct method of making figures with slabs is to construct the body parts out of pieces, and then assemble them (page 65).

A base shape was cut from a slab, and two cylinders were formed for the legs. These were then joined onto the base. A larger piece of clay was cut to form the body and also made into a cylinder. This was placed over the legs, and the legs were very firmly joined on the inside using fingers and a stick. The top of the cylinder was flattened and joined, and a head and neck modelled on firmly. Arms were rolled out and joined, and all the details of clothing, hair and face were completed. Every child had a clear idea before they started about the character and dress of the person they were making. It was developed from their 'Life in the 1940s–1950s' and '1950s–1960s' Topics. It is important when using this method to ensure that no air is trapped inside the work, so when they were completed, small holes were made in the base and a rod pushed up inside the figure to the head and then removed. These pieces were decorated with coloured slips, before being biscuit fired, and glazed with a transparent earthenware glaze to 1140°C.

There are other examples using a cylinder of clay as a basic form, which explore German dress arising out of a European Topic (see page 31).

None of these pieces took much more than around two hours to make, and the 9–11 year old children involved had no previous experience of working in this way.

Viking longboats

This work developed out of a study of Viking life with a class of 7–9 year old children. They had visited the Jorvik Viking Centre in York and had a good first-hand experience of the topic which carried through into the work. These boats are approximately 18 inches (48 cm) long, and were constructed quickly with groups of six children using firm pre-rolled slabs. There was discussion about the shape of the boat and a thin card template made for the sides. The two sides were cut out, and placed onto a slab base forming the boat shape. The joints were reinforced with a coil of clay and firmly modelled. Excess clay around the base was cut away, and slab seats were fixed inside, supported by a piece of vertical slab clay underneath. The figures were modelled and joined on to the seats, and further details added, including food bowls, weapons and shields. They took under two hours to complete, and when finished were covered and allowed to dry slowly to prevent cracking. When biscuit fired, they were painted with stains and glazed with a matt earthenware glaze, fired to 1140°C. They are a useful reminder of the potential for using slabs to make more unusual forms, and of the importance of group work for interaction and learning. The Viking figures which also came out of this project, whilst not as ambitious as the longboats, similarly

'The Beatles' by Amy, Nichola and Sian, aged 10 and Laura, aged 9. Slab construction with modelling, slip decorated, glazed with transparent earthenware glaze to 1140°C.

Below
Viking longboats, group work, children aged 7–9.

used a combination of modelling and slab pieces (see page 102).

At no time should the making methods describes in this book be considered separate and distinct from each other. For the purposes of this book they have been to some extent dealt with separately, but in practice once children understand how clay may be worked, they will use any methods available to them to realise their ideas. It is for the teacher to ensure that they have this experience so that they can fully exploit the potential of clay as an expressive material.

Chapter Seven
Surface Decoration

The wonderful tactile quality of clay leads children instinctively to begin to manipulate the surface of whatever they make. They require no encouragement by the teacher to start to pinch, mark and add on to the surface as a means of developing their ideas, and their readiness to do this gives much of the distinctive character to their work. It is this real vitality and robustness of approach to both the form and surface which is the hallmark of primary claywork, and is something to be encouraged. There are, however, ways in which we as teachers can enrich and broaden this innate enthusiasm: by supplying a wide range of simple tools and by encouraging further experimentation. This applies across the full age range with which we are dealing, and is an essential part of the whole creative process.

The clay which you select is an important part of this process. A fine clay will give sharpness, clarity and smoothness to the drawing or modelling, whereas a grogged clay gives a rich, rough and more ragged quality. Both should be used to provide a rounded experience.

The desire to decorate objects which we make is a basic human characteristic and is prompted by a complex web of attitudes. These range from simply wishing to make something more attractive, to embellishing an object with a subject from everyday experience, or even, as in primitive societies, to endowing an object with religious or magical properties. Children for the most part simply respond to the material in a direct personal way, but there are simple processes by which we can lead them through a variety of decorative techniques and problems.

Drawing

If children are given any implement, they will begin to mark the surface of clay with the same ease with which they draw on paper. The difference is that they are immediately making a low relief image, the quality of which is affected by the way in which the light falls across it. As with drawing on paper, the nature of the mark is determined by the medium or implement used. A pencil will give a different quality from charcoal, and so with clay we need to have available a whole variety of mark-making tools. These can range from needles to pointed sticks, nails, flat pieces of wood, pencils, modelling tools, twigs, combs, kitchen forks, and of course even fingers will be used by little children. As a teacher you need to look around and collect a resource box full of useful mark-making implements for the children to select from. They will, with little encouragement, explore freely with whatever you make available, and this is an important element in building their visual and tactile awareness.

Drawings can be made on flat tiles, or on any of the forms produced as described in previous chapters (coiling, pinching or slabbing), but you must stress with the children that if they draw too deeply they will cut their work apart. I suggest that you tell them not to draw more than half way through the clay, and be prepared to make some repairs early on!

Texture and pattern

We frequently use the words texture and pattern with children in relation to their work and the things which they are looking at, but they are sometimes confused. Texture refers to the roughness or smoothness of a surface, and the ways in which it is articulated, whereas pattern is a decorative design **on** the surface of an object. In practice, of course, they do overlap.

The tactile experience is an essential part of children's understanding of their environment, and they use their hands constantly to explore the world around them. Clay, by its very nature, is probably the most accessible and valuable material in the classroom for children to develop this tactile sense in an exciting and valuable way. Early

Earthenware tiles by Damien, Gavin and Tessa, aged 8. White slip, incised drawing based on Celtic patterns.

work with very young children will simply involve exploration by squeezing, pressing, poking and pinching. They will rapidly move on to modelling, but it is worthwhile encouraging them to spend time finding out what they can do with the surface of the clay, firstly just with their fingers, and then with a wide variety of other objects. Your 'bit box' collection is essential for this. Often the most initially unpromising object will be seized upon by a child to create a new and exciting pattern. Give thought to the clay which you are using. The variations between smooth and grogged clay will influence dramatically the quality of the texture and marks which the children make.

Texture

Working with textures on clay is of course only part of the experience for children. It is essential that their attention is drawn to the surfaces of things around them, both natural and manmade. They should be encouraged to look at, and touch, the surfaces of as wide a variety of things as possible – tree bark, stones and rocks, walls, fabrics, things which are soft and smooth, rough and sharp, even and uneven – as a means of building an awareness of their world.

In addition to marking the clay, impressions can be taken of many surfaces using slabs of clay, provided

that the clay is not too sticky and the surface does not have a very deep texture. This is an exciting process for children because they have to select their surface carefully, but when they remove the clay they have a negative impression which looks very different from the original. This positive-negative concept is of course something which they may know something about through their printmaking activities.

Pattern

Painting shapes and designs on ceramics with coloured slips is a process of decoration which has been used since earliest times to enrich and enliven the form. The ways in which this has been achieved has depended upon the technology available to the potter, but the simplest method has frequently involved using a darker clay over a lighter one and vice versa. This gives enough contrast in even the most primitive firing to be effective. The patterns used can be broadly divided into those which use geometric shapes in various ways – circles, triangles, dots and lines, squares etc., and those which use more obvious elements from the potter's surroundings – flowers, people, animals, fish and so on, depending upon what the potter feels is significant.

It is important to remember that if detailed patterns are going to be painted onto the surface, that surface needs to be fairly flat, because it is very difficult to paint accurately on an undulating surface. Most of the finest historical examples have a smooth surface onto which the pattern has been applied, and this smooth surface is not easy for young children to achieve.

Left
Cheshire Cat by Becky, aged 11. Based on *Alice in Wonderland*. Stoneware with iron oxide decoration, fired to 1260°C.

Below
Triceratops by Helen, aged 7. Earthenware, slip decorated, fired to 1060°C.

Decoration using colour

There are four principal ways in which the colour of the children's work can be changed.

1. Using different coloured clays during making.
2. Painting coloured slips onto the raw clay.
3. Painting underglaze colours onto the biscuit fired (pre-fired) pot.
4. Using coloured glazes.

In practice it is likely that the first two methods will be the most commonly used, in conjunction with a suitable glaze, since underglaze colours tend to be expensive and can be difficult to apply. As always with young children, the simplest and most direct processes tend to be the most successful.

Using different clays together

It is perfectly possible to use different clays together in the same piece, provided that care is taken in their selection. They should ideally have similar wet to dry shrinkage rates to avoid cracking during drying and firing. In practice, clays which are both smooth or both have a similar grog content will work quite well together. This allows, for example, a red earthenware clay to be used with a lighter buff firing stoneware clay giving an interesting light and dark colour contrast to the work. There are a number of examples of this use of mixed clays elsewhere in this book (see photographs on pages 2, 22, 26, 34 and 70).

It is suggested that if, for example, you are applying decorative elements in a grey stoneware clay to red earthenware, that you paint a slip made from the red earthenware clay into the surface before pressing the stoneware clay down. This will help to keep the stoneware clay clean and fresh-looking. Naturally, if you are using earthenware onto stoneware then the reverse is necessary, with a stoneware slip used for joining. Careful working and clean hands will give the best results here, particularly with red earthenware which has a tendency to mark everything.

Painting with coloured slips

This is the easiest and technically most simple method by which children can add colour to their work, and it is used extensively on the examples in this book. By using clay slip to which commercially-produced stains or metal oxides have been added in various proportions, a wide palette of colours can be made available for the children to use. These are brushed onto the raw clay, preferably at the leatherhard stage with soft brushes, and allowed to dry.

There are two problems which need to be considered when children paint slips on to their work. Firstly, if the clay has been allowed to dry too much, there is a danger of breaking off pieces from the model – tails, arms etc., and so, much care and soft brushes are essential. Secondly, if the model is still very damp, it is not easy to get a sufficient thickness onto the surface, and several applications may be needed with time for drying between each layer.

Slips can be applied over each other giving a variety of decorative possibilities, but again it is better if the base colour has dried a little to prevent smudging and blending. Most pottery suppliers have ready-made coloured slips available, but the colour range may be limited. If you have a little time and patience it is perfectly possible to mix your own.

Once decorated, allow the work to dry in the normal way and then biscuit fire. It can then be glazed, usually with a transparent or semi-opaque glaze to bring out the full richness of the slip colour.

Dipping work in slip

It is possible that occasionally you may wish to cover a complete piece or a tile in slip, perhaps as a base colour for further decoration. You obviously need a sufficient quantity in a bucket for this (see Mixing coloured slips on page 84) and there are certain important factors to bear in mind.

1. Make sure that your clay has dried to a soft leatherhard stage.
2. Make sure that the slip has a consistency of single cream. If it is too thick, add water because if it is too thick it may crack off during drying.
3. Remember that the clay will absorb water from the slip and soften, so when it has been dipped, set it aside and leave until it has dried to the point where it can be handled without smudging.
4. Don't dip pieces with a lot of surface detail or thin added modelling as you will cover the detail and the modelling may soften and drop off.

This method is ideal for tiles which can be made quickly using the cutting method described earlier (see pages 57–8). Once they are firmed up, the top surface can then be dipped. As soon as the slip has lost its shine, the children can draw into the surface and/or scrape away parts of the slip to show the clay underneath. If you use a white slip over a red earthenware body, you immediately have a very attractive light and dark design.

Dipping an earthenware tile into slip.

Allowing the excess slip to drain off.

Slip trailing

This traditional process uses a container with a fine nozzle, nowadays a rubber bulb, to paint slip onto a surface. It requires a fair amount of control in order to achieve a design, and a very direct response. This is not something to be recommended for very young children, but with small groups of older children, and some initial practice on the table to develop a feel for the slip trailer it can

Slip trailing using a rubber bulb.

produce exciting results. The problem is knowing when to stop. It requires very careful hand eye coordination for success. You will need plenty of slabs prepared for this work, and the children will need to have looked closely at historical examples before they begin. If they make a mess of their first piece the slip can be sponged off, the clay allowed to dry a little, and then redecorated.

Any topic which touches on 17th and 18th century pottery will involve looking at slip-trailed decoration.

Using resists

The resist process is one in which a water-resistant material is applied to the clay which then prevents the slip or glaze adhering to the clay. This allows for a variety of pattern and colour variations to be achieved. There are two materials which are suitable in the primary situation: paper, and wax emulsion. Each can be applied to the clay surface, which for the best effects should be as flat as possible.

The method is straightforward. Make the clay surfaces, and allow them to firm up. If using wax emulsion (available from pottery suppliers), paint the design onto the surface with a brush and allow to dry. If using paper, select a soft paper (kitchen paper or paper towel is ideal), cut to shape, and using a **little** water and a brush, stick the paper to the clay. Using a soft brush loaded with slip, paint an even layer over the clay and allow to dry. With wax emulsion the resist is immediate, but with paper the slip must be allowed to dry. When it is dry, with a needle or other suitable tool, remove the paper and the design will be revealed. This can be a very exciting and satisfying process for children, who enjoy the element of surprise when they remove the paper to reveal their design. Any slip which has crept under the paper can be gently removed with a scraper.

Mixing coloured slips

Coloured slips are simply liquid clay to which metal oxides or prepared stains have been added in various proportions to give colour of differing strengths. This takes a little time and organisation but once the slips have been made you will have a range of colours which will keep indefinitely in sealed jars.

The method which I use is as follows. You will need these materials and equipment.

Materials and equipment

Powdered ball clay, 10 kg (22 lb)
A bucket with a tight lid, 5 gallon
A spare bucket
A balloon whisk for mixing
An 80s mesh sieve, and a stiff brush
As many small containers with lids as possible, preferably plastic
Prepared stains in a range of colours, say 100 g (approx. 4 oz.) of each
A measuring jug
Measuring spoons

Method

1. Add 20 pints of water to the bucket, and gently add the ball clay to it, keeping it stirred and making as little dust as possible.
2. Using the whisk and your hand, mix the slip to an even consistency, and then sieve it through the 80s mesh sieve into the spare bucket using the stiff brush.

This basic slip without stains or oxides can be used to give a white or cream slip.

Figure of a lion, English, 1790–1800. Decorated with high temperature underglaze colours. *Courtesy of the Hanley Museum, Stoke on Trent.*

3. Using the measuring jug pour 7 fl.oz (200 ml) of slip into each of the jars.

4. It is normal practice to dry weigh ingredients for ceramic recipes, but since it is unlikely that the average school will have accurate gram scales, measuring spoons are a practical alternative. Stains are added in the range of 5%–15% dry weight depending upon the strength of colour required. Use your judgement here but as a guide you could add ½ a tablespoon to the first container, 1 tablespoon to the next, and 1½ to a third. This will give a range of colours from light to dark depending on the stain.

5. Put the lids on the containers and give them a very good shake. Ideally they should be sieved through a small cup lawn, but for our purposes this method of mixing usually works.

6. Keep an accurate record as you proceed for future reference, and make sure that each container is securely labelled.

As the children use up particular colours you can quite easily top up the jars with slip and stain, provided that the main bucket of slip is kept sealed and not allowed to dry out.

Remember that stains are not paint. The colour comes from a chemical reaction in the kiln, and the true brightness of a colour will not develop until it has been fired. Glaze over the top gives the final brilliance to the slip.

Using metal oxides

If commercially-produced stains are not available, then there are a range of metal oxides which can be used to give colour to your slips, but since they vary considerably in their colouring strength you need to be careful about the percentages used. The following is a guide for a number of different oxides.

Chromium oxide	1–7%	Grey green
Copper carbonate	1–7%	Green
Red iron oxide	3–15%	Cream to brown and black
Cobalt oxide	0.5–5%	Blue
Manganese dioxide	5–15%	Browns
Nickel oxide	2–5%	Grey browns

Note particularly how little cobalt oxide you need for a strong blue.

On a health and safety note keep the stains and oxides securely locked away, and avoid inhaling dust or ingesting when using them.

All these coloured slips should be applied to the raw clay, preferably when it has firmed up a little, and before it has gone dry for reasons already explained.

Using underglaze colours

Underglaze colours, as the name suggests, are painted onto the biscuit clay before the final glaze is applied. This traditionally was done by mixing the colour with oil, and required a further firing to fix it to the clay. Recently there have been developments which allow for painting with special mediums and then glazing directly over the top, but realistically, in the primary situation, this requires so much control and technical understanding that the use of slips has to be the first option, not only in practical and educational terms, but also in relation to cost.

Decorating with glazes

The technical aspects of using glazes will be dealt with in more detail in Chapter 9, but it is worth mentioning at this point that by using a number of different coloured glazes painted onto the work some very effective results can be achieved. There are two important points to be noted here. Firstly, the thickness of the application will affect the colour of the final result, and secondly, you must be sure that the glazes which you use all melt at the same temperature. Nevertheless, if you have biscuit fired the children's work without slip, and decide that some colour is needed, the use of glazes is the only way in which you will get a result.

We now move on to building and using kilns, and biscuit firing.

Chapter Eight
Firing Clay

Why fire?

For children to understand fully the change which occurs when clay turns to ceramic, it is important if possible that they experience it at first hand. It is a most exciting process, and one which even professional potters find continually fascinating. To commit your most precious work to a fire, and then to have to wait to see the results builds an anticipation and tension which is quite unique to the craft. For children to see this happen is to experience the concept of change in an immediate way, and relates directly to the science curriculum, particularly energy transfers, and reversible and irreversible change. In this case, irreversible. There are also some wonderful historical links with primitive kilns, in that all the Iron and Bronze Age, Roman and Medieval pottery which we see in museums was fired in simple pit or clamp kilns using wood as a fuel. In parts of Africa today large handbuilt pots are still fired in bonfire kilns using brushwood as a fuel.

The most common question from teachers who are contemplating using clay is 'What do I do if I haven't got a kiln?' The answer is 'Let the children use clay anyway'. For most children of this age range there is so much educational value to be gained from the experience of working with the material that not to give them this experience because of the lack of a kiln is, I believe, a missed

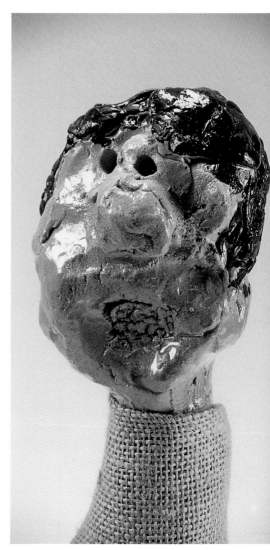

Viking puppet head by Matthew, aged 7. Decorated using underglaze stains with a transparent earthenware glaze.

opportunity. This said, however, the ability to fire the work, to make it permanent and to give them something to take home adds a whole new dimension to their education and if you are determined, it is often possible to use a kiln in another school, a teacher's centre, or perhaps cajole a friendly local potter to help.

There are, however, simple ways in which clay can be turned into pottery without sophisticated and expensive kilns, and the building of sawdust, pit, and bonfire kilns are detailed later in this chapter. Building and firing such kilns does require some time, effort and organisation by the teacher but the excitement of the process and the learning which takes place as a result is quite special and unique. It is tempting for inexperienced teachers to feel that this is beyond them. However, in practice it is quite simple if you are determined to try it, and it always provides a unique and memorable shared experience. Don't be put off by not knowing! For any firing to be successful, it is important that the teacher knows what is happening to the clay during firing and to control this as much as possible. There will, as every potter knows, be disappointments when work is taken from the kiln, but there is always that element of the unexpected, and when really lovely work emerges all the effort suddenly becomes worthwhile. It is a moment which all of us 'children', young and old, never forget.

What happens?

The children will be aware of the change from soft plastic clay to hard but brittle dry clay through their experience of working with it. When it is heated, clay goes through a series of gradual changes. The first, and most important, is what is called the water smoking stage. This occurs early in the firing when the water still remaining in the clay due to humidity is driven off. This is a critical time because if it happens too quickly the water turns to steam and blows the clay apart. This problem has been mentioned frequently elsewhere in this book, particularly with reference to the thickness of the clay and the grog content. If the clay is more open, it is easier for the steam to escape. In practice, so long as the temperature rise is slow up to around 200°C (392°F) or a little higher the work will survive.

Once this stage has passed, the temperature can be increased steadily to the required top temperature. Between 350°C and 700°C the clay turns increasingly to pottery, becoming steadily harder and harder although it will still be porous. By 600°C it can no longer be returned to the plastic state.

Different clays mature at different temperatures. Maturing means that the clay has reached its optimum strength and vitrification. Most clays have quite a wide range of maturity, perhaps 40°C or more, and will still be slightly porous at this point. This applies rather more to earthenware clays than to stoneware, but for the type of work which our children make, it is not really important. However, if a clay is taken beyond its vitrification point, it will start to deform, and if you are unfortunate enough, for example, to overfire an earthenware kiln, you might find that the clay has completely collapsed or even melted! Such occurrences are fortunately extremely rare. I will now explain how you might fire the children's work successfully, starting with very primitive methods and moving on to using more sophisticated electric kilns.

Left top
Preparing the base to take the boxes of
warmed pots.

Centre
20 minutes later, the whole school watching
their pots being fired.

Bottom
1 hour later, the pots emerge from the ashes.

quantity of wood from an enthusiastic
parent, the temperature reached at least
1200°C in the middle because the
stoneware clay vitrified and the pots held
water afterwards. The excitement of the
children when the fire began to die down
and they saw their pots emerging from
the ashes was a very special and
memorable moment for all of us. The
whole firing usually only takes around
two hours at the most from start to
finish.

As I have already mentioned this
firing method is still used in Africa and
elsewhere to produce pots for use. It is a
particularly dramatic and immediate
way of firing clay, although not without
some risks.

Pit or trench firing

This type of kiln, which as I have
mentioned before was used in Medieval
and Roman times, requires more effort in
both construction and firing than a
sawdust kiln. As before, you will need a
suitable area of secure open ground
where it can be dug and built, plenty of
willing helpers, and a good supply of dry
wood in short lengths to fire it.
Depending upon how large you build it,
you will also need a suitable quantity of
old bricks, a length of metal pipe or a
clay drainage pipe, and some corrugated
iron or old kiln shelves to cover the fire
trench.

Construction

Begin by digging a trench in the ground
approximately 5 feet long, 2 feet wide,
and 1 foot deep (150 cm × 60 cm ×
30 cm). Make it about 6 inches (15 cm)
wider where you will be putting the pots
to give space for the flames to move
around them, and slope the other end to
give access to the firebox.

Line the bottom of the trench with

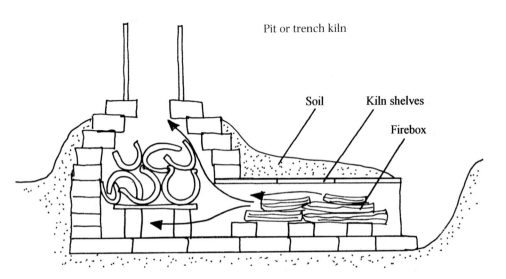

Pit or trench kiln

Soil   Kiln shelves

Firebox

Above
Base of kiln laid out in an excavated flower
bed.

Left
Firebox and chamber under construction.

of the kiln. Place some bricks crossways
across the fire trench to support the
wood while it burns and allow space for
the ash to fall, then cover the fire trench
with corrugated iron or shelves, and put
some soil over the top for insulation.
Place your pots inside the kiln on top of
each other, making sure that the stack is
stable and that there is room around the
outside for the heat and flames to
circulate. Close in the kiln walls at the
top and place the chimney on top,
making sure that it is secure. Leave a
spyhole in the wall so that you, and
more importantly the children, can see
what is happening during the firing. Use
spare soil to cover the sides of the kiln
chamber and provide additional
insulation.

bricks, and build up the sides, backfilling
behind the walls. Lay some $\frac{1}{2}$ inch
(12 mm) iron bars across the kiln area to
support your pots, or alternatively build
a platform of bricks on which to stand
them, and continue to build up the walls

Above
Kiln almost complete and covered with soil.

Below
Children watching the firing in progress.

Firing

This firing will take time, so start it early in the morning to allow the children to see the firing at the end before they go home.

You can pack the kiln with either soft fired biscuit pots or with raw clay pieces. If the pots are still raw clay, however, it is essential for the reasons explained earlier, to be very careful early on in the firing. Light a very small fire with paper and small pieces of wood in the entrance to the firebox, and keep it small for several hours. The chimney will provide a draw for the heat and gradually warm the pots. Don't be tempted to rush this stage or you will blow all the pots to pieces. Three hours warming is not too long a time for this stage, and if the ground is very wet, you might warm the kiln the previous day with a small fire, and then close off the entrance overnight with bricks to let it dry out gently.

Once the watersoaking stage has finished, you can gradually introduce more wood and build up the fire. You should easily reach a temperature of 1000°C in this kiln, and if you are able to fire it longer even 1150°C is possible. The temperature can be judged by looking at the colour through the spyhole, or by using a thermocouple with an indicator if you have one available. For our purposes the extact temperature is not critical because there are no glazes to melt in a firing like this.

The cooling process must be taken slowly, so once the firing has finished, close up the firebox with bricks and soil to prevent unwanted draughts, and cover the top of the chimney also with bricks or a piece of kiln shelf. The next day you can open the firebox and uncover the chimney top to allow the cooling to continue, and with luck you will be able to take out the pots later that day.

Once you have built a kiln like this, it can be covered with polythene or corrugated metal and used over and over again. Local timber merchants will often give scrap wood for use in school, and so you are set up with free firings, and all the value of direct experience for the children.

Electric kilns

After the excitement of sawdust, bonfire and pit firing, electric kilns are rather tame. However, they do have a major advantage for teachers in that they require virtually no supervision during the firing, which means that precious time can be used for other things. Their disadvantage is that the children cannot experience the changes to their work at first hand. Nevertheless, they are an important piece of equipment for any school which uses clay regularly, and although the initial cost is quite high, the running costs are low, and the life of a kiln, if used properly, is long. I am currently using an electric kiln which is now thirty years old and still firing beautifully.

There are now available two basic types of electric kiln: front-loading and top-loading. Recent advances in technology have made these kilns very efficient in use, both with controls, and with the materials from which they are made. Most kilns now combine special refractory bricks with ceramic fibre (a development from the space programme) which means that more of the heat is used in firing the pots, and less in heating the kiln lining. There are slight advantages in having a front loading kiln because it is little easier to pack and involves less bending over, but many schools now use top loading kilns which tend to be cheaper to purchase initially. The differences in methods in packing are covered later.

Siting

Regulations regarding the siting of kilns in school have to be complied with, and these require placing the kiln in a room separate from the classroom, with adequate ventilation from windows or extractor fan, and often with a secure cage around. There should be a space of at least 6 inches (15 cm) from any wall with adequate room for servicing, and there should be a minimum $2\frac{1}{2}$ foot (75 cm) space above the kiln. There should be no combustible materials in the vicinity. Despite the insulation, the outside casing can become very warm during a firing, around 140°C, and children need to be kept well away. The controls also need to be away from the reach of children for obvious reasons. All modern kilns are now supplied with a door interlock, which prevents the kiln from being opened during the firing, and which isolates the electricity supply. If you are proposing to purchase a kiln for your school, check with the manufacturer that it complies with legal requirements, and check also with your local education office regarding the latest regulations. These tend to be upgraded periodically, and you need to be sure before you purchase.

Size

Electric kilns can be supplied in a range of different sizes, normally calculated on the capacity of the kiln chamber in cu. ft. These can start at one cu.ft and go on to kilns which you can walk into! The size for your school will depend upon a number of factors. Firstly, how much claywork will you be undertaking, remembering that when you have a kiln you will want to use it? Secondly, do you have a suitable and sufficient electricity supply? It is better to have a kiln which is too large than too small, otherwise you will be constantly packing and unpacking children's work. Most of the work in this book has been fired in a kiln of around $4\frac{1}{2}$ cu. ft. which is a nice size to

take a batch of work from an average primary class. It is also large enough to take more ambitious pieces from groups of older children. Lastly, what temperature will you be firing to? In the past manufacturers made kilns for earthenware and stoneware to different specifications. If you have an older kiln, you need to check what temperature it was designed for. Nowadays many kilns are made to fire over the whole range up to 1300°C, but check catalogues carefully because if you only wish to fire to say 1200°C the lower temperature specification will save money.

Controls

To fire an electric kiln we need to know two things. First, what the temperature is inside the chamber during the firing and second, how much energy we are putting into the kiln. The temperature is measured with a thermocouple which sticks into the chamber and is connected to an indicator. The indicator might be a needle moving across a dial, or a digital readout. The energy input control could be a simple switch, high, medium, low, a dial calibrated to 100, or an electronic programmer which allows you to set the rate of climb of the kiln in degrees per hour. None of these are difficult to use by even a complete novice. The most important control is the cut-off when the kiln has reached temperature. This is set at the start of the firing for either biscuit or glost, and when the kiln reaches temperature it either switches off immediately, or if you have programmed it to do so, holds the temperature for a period, say half an hour, and then switches off. This is useful when glaze firing to allow the glaze to mature and smooth out on the pots. (See Chapter Nine, Using Cones.) It is essential in my experience for any kiln in a school to have good controls, as this will avoid the need for teachers to stand over the kiln at the end of a firing. Once you have got used to your particular kiln, you will find that it takes hardly any time to pack and fire.

Packing an electric kiln for a biscuit firing

There are no difficulties in packing a kiln, provided you observe certain simple methods. I will describe how to pack a front-loading kiln first.

1. Look at the works to be packed and check two things: a) Is it dry? and b) How tall is it? Select work which is all roughly the same height.
2. Place three props on the bottom shelf about $\frac{1}{2}$ inch (12 mm) taller than the work.
3. Put the greenware onto the shelf, packing the pieces so that they touch if necessary. This can be done at biscuit stage. Work such as bowls etc. can be placed inside each other without harm.

Tortoise by Sarah, aged 6. Earthenware, honey glaze.

4. Carefully place a kiln shelf onto the props, without touching the sides of the kiln or elements. If it is a bit wobbly, lift the shelf a fraction and replace it.
5. Place three more props onto that shelf, making sure that they are directly above those below, and continue placing greenware into the kiln. If the kiln has two stacks of shelves, it is best to pack a front-loading kiln from the back. This avoids damaging work in the front as you reach across.
6. Finally close and lock the door, and remove the bung to allow any moisture to escape early in the firing.

Packing a top-loading kiln follows the same procedures, except that you need to check very much more carefully how tall your work is. Select the props for your tallest piece before you begin to pack, because when you place the shelf down into the kiln you cannot see easily how high the work is and it is easy to damage tall pieces. Similarly, when you are placing props on the shelf, you need to feel around the shelf with your fingers to locate the props above the ones below. Once you have done it a few times, it becomes automatic and very easy.

Firing a biscuit kiln

This is the firing where most work is lost if you are not careful. Below is a graph showing a typical biscuit firing together with an Earthenware Glaze schedule.

You can see that the early part of the biscuit firing is taken very slowly, particularly if there is thick-walled work in the kiln. I would suggest that 3–4 hours to 200°C is a minimum rate of climb. In practice, you will probably turn the kiln on very low and leave it overnight to gently heat up. Then in the morning you can turn up the control switch to around 50% input, and when the kiln has reached 500–600°C it can be turned on to full power. Once the firing has finished, leave the kiln to cool until it is below 200°C before you open the bung or crack the door.

Once it is cold, the work can be removed and decisions taken about whether to glaze, or just to leave it in the biscuit state. At this point the work will still be porous, and the surface appearance rather dull and bland. If the purpose of the particular project was mainly concerned with giving the children experience of handling clay, then you may legitimately decide that making it permanent to give them something to take home is as far as you need to go as an educational experience. In my experience this is often the case with very young children, and by the time the work has dried and been put through the kiln they have often forgotten which piece is theirs. They never forget the experience of handling clay though, and the awareness of change from soft to hard is a central concept in ceramics.

Firing Graph

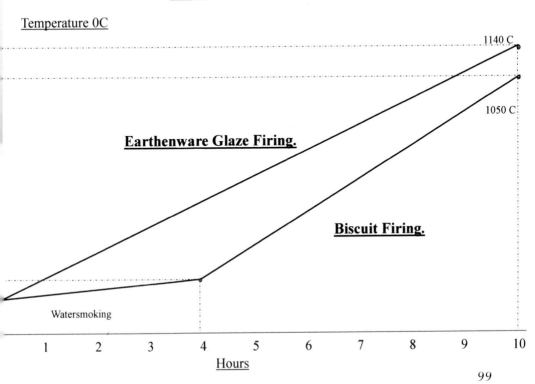

Temperature 0C

1140 C

1050 C

Earthenware Glaze Firing.

Biscuit Firing.

Watersmoking

1   2   3   4   5   6   7   8   9   10

Hours

Chapter Nine
Glazes and Glaze Firing

Teachers have differing views regarding the educational value of glaze firing the work of young children, and these views tend to vary according to the age of the class. On the one hand, there is the belief that the important learning takes place, for the most part, when children are using the clay and that once this experience is completed we need go no further. There is of course some merit in this attitude, particularly with the younger age groups. There is also the view that by taking their work through the different stages of biscuit and glazing, that learning is extended and developed. Links are made for the children between their work and the ceramics surrounding them in their daily lives, and also as has been previously mentioned, between different areas of the curriculum. There is no doubt in my mind that whatever their age there is an immense satisfaction, pride and value in children being able to show a piece of glazed work to parents and friends. It is the culmination of the whole experience, but ultimately whether to glaze fire has to be a matter of personal choice and circumstances.

For those teachers who have a kiln in the school, or who have access to one, this chapter covers in a simple way how to complete the glaze firing process. It is outside the scope of this book to attempt to cover the formulation and mixing of glazes, which is a much more specialist and technical area, and it is also for the most part inappropriate, given the demands which it makes on primary teachers in terms of time and resources. For those teachers who wish to develop experience in this area there is considerable information available in the literature devoted to the craft potter. For the purposes of this chapter, it is assumed that all glaze firing will take place in an electric kiln since this is the usual facility available in schools.

Why glaze?

The pot which emerges from the biscuit kiln, whilst it is hard, has a dull, bland and lifeless surface, and will still be porous. By taking it through the glaze firing we can produce a surface which is bright and colourful, and which will hold liquids. The finished surface will vary in quality depending upon the glaze, giving a range of qualities, from dry to matt, shiny, clear and opaque. The application of a glaze over coloured slips and stains will also make the colours of these much richer and more vibrant. Probably most important of all will be the change in the tactile quality of the piece, from the rather rough and dry surface of biscuit, to the smoothness of glaze.

What is a glaze?

In essence a glaze is a type of glass, which when it is heated, binds to the clay to form an impervious layer. It is made from a number of ingredients, most of which are naturally occurring minerals, or which are made from processed minerals. These are blended together and mixed with water to hold them in suspension, and it is in this creamy liquid state that they are used. The range of minerals found in glazes is very wide. They may include ground granite, limestone, flint and quartz, and clays including ball clay and china clay as well as metal oxides for colouring, such as iron, copper, cobalt and manganese. At lower earthenware temperatures the glaze will contain a high percentage of frit. Since it is likely in the primary school that much of the firing will take place at an earthenware temperature, I should explain what frits are. At these lower temperatures some of the materials which are used to make glazes are difficult or dangerous to handle. These include lead, potassium, borax and sodium. By mixing them with other materials, melting them and pouring this melt into water (thus hardening it) and then grinding it down, it is rendered much safer to use. It is from these frits (the ground down state) that suppliers produce a variety of low solubility glazes, and provided that their guidelines are followed, particularly in relation to using them in combination with underglaze colours and stains there should be no problem.

Choosing your glaze

Suppliers catalogues often contain a dazzling array of glazes for use in school, and it can be very difficult for a beginner to decide what to order. I would suggest that your first decision is what temperature you wish to fire to. If you have a kiln which can reach stoneware temperatures of around 1250°C or more, then your choice is whether to order glazes for both earthenware and stoneware, or just one. Remember that your colour range with stoneware is not as bright or as varied as that at lower temperatures, and if this is what you require, then an earthenware glaze is an obvious choice. You will then need to consider which particular range of glazes to use. These often vary both in maturing temperature and in the glaze effect. With earthenware you may have some glazes maturing at 1046°C (1915°F) and others at 1101°C (2014°F). It is important that you only use glazes which mature at the same temperature in each firing. For practical reasons it is advisable to settle on one temperature for all your glazes and avoid the risks of overfiring and losing work.

As a start, I would recommend that you order a quantity of clear transparent gloss glaze, some matt clear glaze, and some opaque white glaze. These will give a simple variety of surface qualities, and allow some flexibility in the ways in which you use slips, stains and oxides to colour the work.

These prepared glazes are usually available as a powder from the supplier, and this is the cheapest way to purchase larger quantities of glaze. Liquid brush-on glazes are also available in a whole variety of colours, and you may decide to purchase smaller quantities of these to use in conjunction with your bulk glazes. They have the advantage that they are ready mixed, and because you normally use them straight from the bottle there is little or no waste. Make sure that they are compatible with your base glazes by checking with the supplier.

Mixing batch glazes

You will need a number of 3–5 gallon buckets with good tight fitting lids to mix and store your glaze. You need to buy enough powdered glaze to mix a reasonable batch at a time, and also to have some in reserve, because it is likely that you will use these base glazes to dip the work into. It can be very annoying to find that you don't have enough glaze in which to dip larger pieces. The ratio of water to powder will vary a little according to the glaze type, but as a guide 1 kg–1 pint of water, or 2 lb–20 fl.oz can be used as an approximate measure. The weighed powder should be slipped gently into the water. Try to avoid creating dust in the air. The slop should be thoroughly mixed, and then passed through an 80s mesh sieve into another bucket. The glaze consistency should be as near to a pouring single cream as possible. When the glaze is mixed, make sure that you fix a label to the bucket to avoid mistakes in use, and keep it tightly sealed to avoid evaporation.

Viking lady with table, dog and fire by Natalie, aged 7.

Applying glazes

The ways in which you put glaze onto a piece will affect the appearance after firing. The thickness and evenness of the glaze, and the effects of one glaze over another, perhaps combined with slips underneath will give a wide variety of finished surfaces. It is this potential element of unpredictability in all firings which makes it such an exciting process, and is one which captivates everyone who works with clay.

Glaze can be applied to biscuit ware by brushing, pouring, dipping and spraying. The latter requires specialist spraying equipment and an extractor with a filter, and so is not likely to be used in school. The most common methods for primary use will be brushing and dipping. The aim is to get as even a layer as possible onto the surface, and with a thickness of approximately $\frac{1}{16}$ inch (1 mm).

Brushing glaze

This requires good soft brushes which will hold a quantity of glaze, and careful application. You will find that several layers will be needed to build up a sufficient thickness, and the glaze should be applied in different directions onto the piece to achieve an even layer. If you are using prepared brush-on glazes in a range of colours to decorate the work, you could either glaze the piece first with a base glaze and then decorate over the top, or work the other way by brushing coloured glaze on first, and then putting say a clear glaze over that. The problem with brushing glaze is the possible unevenness of the surface. Since much children's work is modelled and fairly complicated in the surface treatment, it can be extremely difficult to get an even layer onto the piece.

Dipping

This is by far the quickest and most effective way of glazing complicated pieces, but of course it does require a good quantity of glaze – hence the buckets of base glaze. The work is simply dipped into the glaze, held there for a second or two, and then taken out, shaken gently, and placed down onto a surface to dry. This might sound simple, and it is, but there are certain things to watch out for.

Firstly, try not to get glaze on the bottom of the piece. This will have to be removed later, and that can be tedious and time consuming. Secondly, if the piece is too awkward to hold with one hand, use both hands, and if you have left finger marks on the glaze, just touch them up with a brush after you put the piece down. Always make sure that you have somewhere to put the work down before you dip it, or you will find yourself wandering around with a dripping piece frantically trying to clear a space. This is particularly important with children when they are glazing, and an organized sequence of actions will help to avoid problems with a large group. If, by chance, the work slips and falls into the glaze bucket, and it does happen, just take it out quickly, and wipe it carefully underneath when it has dried.

Pouring

This method of glazing is useful when you only have a small quantity of glaze, or when you need to glaze the inside of a pot form. The work needs to be held over the bucket and the glaze poured from a jug as evenly as possible. Every piece will present a different problem in the way the glaze runs over the form, and you will need to use your ingenuity here.

Glazing a pot requires pouring a quantity of glaze inside first, twirling it around and then pouring it out. The pot is then dipped into the glaze upside down for a few seconds, removed, and set down. If there are any areas inside which are still unglazed, they can be touched up with a brush afterwards. It is very difficult to get an even layer of glaze on a piece by pouring, and most of the time this method should be reserved for glazing the insides of pots only.

Wiping glaze from biscuitware

No matter how careful you and your children are when you glaze, it is inevitable that there will be some glaze left on the bottom of some of the pieces. It is essential that this is removed before firing, otherwise, when it melts it will stick quite wonderfully to the kiln shelf! You will then have no choice but to knock it off with a hammer and chisel! So, using a moist sponge, make sure that all traces of glaze are removed from any part of the piece which will touch the

kiln shelf. In addition, wipe the sides to a minimum of $\frac{1}{8}$ inch (4 mm) from the bottom to provide a space in case the glaze runs a little in the firing. With a known runny glaze this space may need to be greater still. This process of cleaning can be very tedious, particularly with the modelled work from young children, but it is worth taking time over, since kiln shelves are expensive to replace.

Testing

Before using glazes for the first time it is important that you test them, together with any colours you are planning to use, to ensure that they work at your temperature. You can use a tile or small spare pot for this, and the little time which it takes can save the heartache that would ensue if a whole batch of work were spoiled. Put the glaze onto the test piece both as a thick and a thin layer to give a true guide to how it will behave in use.

Packing a glaze kiln

The method of packing a glaze kiln is nearly identical with that of a biscuit kiln described earlier, with the following slight changes.

1. Handle the work more carefully when placing it into the kiln. Try not to knock glaze off the work, and if you do, remove it from the kiln shelf, and touch up the piece with a brush and fresh glaze.

Slab pots by children aged 10–11. Based on work of contemporary potter Alison Britton. Raku clay, decorated with applied shapes and underglaze colours. Some pieces were left unglazed.

2. Double check every piece underneath to make sure that it is clean.
3. Make sure that there is a gap of at least $\frac{3}{8}$ inch (10 mm) between each piece to prevent them from sticking together in the firing.
4. If you are using cones as a firing guide, place them in the kiln, and check that you can see them through the spyhole.

Using cones

I have mentioned cones earlier, and you will also have seen them referred to in suppliers catalogues. They are small pieces of ceramic material, specially formulated to bend after a certain amount of heat work. They do not measure temperature, but give an accurate indication of how your glaze is maturing. This can vary from firing to firing, depending upon how fast or how slow you fire, and how much work is in the kiln. Every kiln behaves a little differently, and a cone is the only accurate way to check what is

happening. Normally two cones are used in each firing, one for the optimum temperature, and one below to give a warning that the firing is almost finished. For example, if your glaze matures at Cone 04, 1060°C (1940°F), you would also put in Cone 05, 1046°C (1915°F) as a guard cone.

Firing a glaze kiln

In many ways this is more straightforward than a biscuit firing because there is no need for a watersmoking period (see Chapter Eight, the firing graph on page 99). You simply set the programmer, or controls to full on, making sure that whatever cut off temperature switch you have is also set, and leave the kiln to fire. If you are checking the firing with cones, you may need to plan your firing to end when you are able to watch it, but this is likely to be a fairly rare occurrence in the average school. You may just use the cones as a

Cones, before and after firing.

guide to what has happened, and check them afterwards. When the firing is finished, let the kiln cool at its own pace, and don't be tempted to open it until it has dropped to below 150°C. This is important with glossy earthenware glazes, which can start to craze if they are subjected to a draught of cold air. Then all that is left is that exciting moment of unpacking and discovery – an event which never loses its magic.

Health and safety

Basic precautions in handling and using ceramic materials have been mentioned earlier, but in relation to glaze materials the following should be strictly observed.

1. Avoid creating dust when mixing glazes from powder – preferably do it outside of the classroom, never when the children are present, and wear a mask.
2. Wipe any spilled glaze on boards or tables with a sponge, never a brush.
3. Avoid ingesting glaze materials and colours.
4. Encourage children to wash their hands thoroughly after any glazing activity.
5. Keep glaze buckets well-sealed and labelled, and raw materials safely stored away.

George Harrison by Nichola, aged 10.

Chapter Ten
Moving Forward

It has been my intention with this book to try to provide a practical and theoretical basis for using clay in the primary school. The children's works which have been included are just a few examples of some of the ways the material can be used. Since clay offers an almost unlimited potential for exploring a wide range of subjects, it is clearly impossible within the scope of a book such as this to suggest how every subject could be treated. In any event, such an approach can quickly become prescriptive and narrow, and one of the joys with clay in the hands of young children is the unexpected creative response which seems to happen every time they use it.

The basic working methods of modelling, coiling, carving, pinching, forming with slabs, decorating and firing have all been explained, and some of the ways in which each of them can be developed have been suggested. It has to be for the individual teacher to consider what will be the most effective way of developing this practical aspect with his or her particular group of children. It also has to relate to the stimulus or idea which is to be used as a starting point for the work. When making these decisions I suggest that the processes described are not approached as discrete areas, but that you consider whether they can be combined – for example, modelling and slab forms, or coil pots with slip decoration. Start with your subject or idea, and decide what will be the most valuable way of approaching it. The questions in Chapter One should help to focus your planning.

Display

All primary teachers have their own approach to display in the classroom, and it is outside the remit of this book to deal in detail with this subject. It has to be recognised, however, that sensitive and thoughtful display of the finished work is a constant reminder of the learning which has taken place, and a celebration of the children's achievements. With this in mind, the following suggestions are offered as guidelines.

1. Give the work space. If you have a lot of pieces don't try to show them all, but make a selection so that individual pieces can be seen to best advantage.
2. Vary the spaces between pieces. Some can be grouped in two's and three's whilst others can stand on their own.
3. Vary the heights. Use boxes of different sizes to change the way pieces are seen.
4. Consider the background. Choose neutral colours which are sympathetic to the colours of the finished work, rather than bright contrasts.
5. Minimise risks. There is always a

danger that work will be damaged, so try to place it somewhere away from major movement in the room. Whether the work is to be handled is an important question, and one which has to be answered according to circumstances. The risks of children damaging each other's work is ever present, and the work will inevitably tempt a tactile response.

Visiting artists

There are schemes in many areas, both formal and informal, whereby placements can be organised with artists and craftspeople to work in schools. These can be for short, intense periods with a focus on a particular project, for example a mural. They can also work over a more extended period involving, say, a day a week. Whatever the arrangement or focus, their value is immense. Both children and teachers gain from the additional expertise and insights such practitioners bring to the school, and from the general enrichment in learning. You might explore whether there is a potter in your area who would be willing to join you for a while and help to develop this work with your children.

Hippo by Ross, aged 7. Earthenware, stoneware teeth, honey glaze, fired to 1140°C.

Using museums

There is no doubt that many local museums can provide a valuable and important resource for our work with clay. As I have mentioned earlier, much of what we know about past cultures comes from their pottery artefacts. For children to begin to understand their own culture and time, they need to be able to place it in the context of the past. There has been a steady improvement in many museums over the years in making their collections more accessible and interesting for primary children, and many have appointed education officers to assist in this. If children are to make the most of such a visit, then you need to plan carefully, and provide a focus for their observation and learning. Many museums provide worksheets and questionnaires to assist in this, but if not, you will need to consider some of the following questions if you are to make the most of the time.

Are the displays easy to see, well lit, and with appropriate labels for your children?

If you are focusing on pottery, these questions might be useful.

What is it made of?
How was it made?
How is it decorated?

What was it used for?
How was it used?
How old is it? How do you know?
Where was it made/found?
What similar objects were made before or after your object, and how are they different?
Are there parts of it which you like or dislike, and why?

It may be that there are artefacts which can be handled by the children, and if this is possible you should take full advantage of the opportunity. There is nothing quite like handling work for a complete experience.

Conclusion

It is a function of art eduction to help children to make sense of their experiences: tactile, visual, emotional and imaginative, and to understand and appreciate not just their own environment, but the historical and cultural context which has produced it. In exploring the visual arts they begin to develop a personal language and skills which relate to a whole range of learning situations, and which are likely to become part of the individual's vocabulary for life. It is my belief that clay, in all its aspects, is an integral part of this learning.

Bibliography

There is an extensive body of research and information in the fields of both art education and ceramics which relate to this book, and the following provides some initial reference to further reading in these areas. They are not intended to be either prescriptive or exhaustive, but to suggest sources of further information which may assist teachers working with this material.

Background reading

Jameson, K., *Junior School Art*, Studio Vista, 1973.

Jameson, K., *Pre-school and Infant Art*, Studio Vista, 1968.

Lancaster, J. (ed.), *Art, Craft and Design in the Primary School*, NSEAD, 1986.

Read, H., *Education through Art*, Faber, 1956.

Taylor, R., *Educating for Art*, Longman, 1986.

Topal, C.W., *Children, Clay and Sculpture*, Davis, 1983.

Some specialised books about Ceramics

Cooper, E., *Glazes*, Batsford, 1992.

Fraser, H., *Ceramic Faults and their Remedies*, A&C Black, 1986.

Fraser, H., *The Electric Kiln (A User's Manual)*, A&C Black, 1994.

Gregory, I., *Kiln Building*, A&C Black, 1995.

Hamer, F. & J., *A Potter's Dictionary*, A&C Black (London), University of Pennsylvania Press, 1986.

Nigrosh, Leon, *Low Fire*, Davis Publications, Inc., 1980.

Nigrosh, Leon, *Sculpting Clay*, Davis Publications, Inc., 1992.

Perryman, J., *Smoke-fired Pottery*, A&C Black, 1995.

Rawson, P., *Ceramics*, University of Pennsylvania Press, 1984.

Sapiro, Maurice, *Clay: Hand Building*, Davis Publications, Inc., 1979.

List of Suppliers

UK

Bath Potters' Supplies
2 Dorset Close
East Twerton, Bath BA2 3RF
Tel. 01225–337046

Briar Wheels and Supplies Ltd.
Whitsbury Road, Fordingbridge
Hants, SP6 1NQ
Tel. 01425–52991

Reward-Clayglaze
Talbot Road
Ricksmanworth, Herts. WD3 1HW
Tel. 01923–770127

Potclays Ltd.
Brickkiln Lane
Etruria, Stoke-on-Trent ST4 7BP
Tel. 01782–219816

Potterycrafts/Reward-Clayglaze Ltd.
Campbell Road
Stoke-on-Trent ST4 4ET
Tel. 01782–272444.

US

A.R.T. Studio Clay Co.
1555 Louis Avenue
Elk Grove Village, IL 60007

American Art Clay Co., Inc.
4717 West Sixteenth Street
Indianapolis, IN 46222

Amherst Potters Supply Inc.
47 East Street
Hadley, MA 01035

Continental Clay Co.
1101 Stinson Blvd. North East
Minneapolis, MN 55413

Georgies Ceramic & Clay Co.
756 North East Lombard
Portland, OR 97211

Texas Pottery Supply
P.O. Box 161305
801 D Airway Drive
Fort Worth, TX 76106

Index